MW01181192

JUMBO JACK'S COOKBOOKS
AUDUBON MEDIA CORPORATION
301 BROADWAY • AUDUBON, IA 50025
1-800-798-2635

THE
HUNTING
IN THE
NUDE
COOKBOOK

by

Bruce Carlson

**HEARTS 'N TUMMIES
COOKBOOK COMPANY**
3544 Blakslee St.
Wever, IA 52658
800-571-BOOK

A Dinky Division of Quixote Press

i

TABLE OF CONTENTS

INDEX TO RECIPES

FOREWORD

Bruce Carlson asked me to say something nice about this book back here. I will, too, if I can think of something.

Meanwhile, my personal opinion is that he's been sleeping with his head too close to the campfire.

But, if you want to learn anything about hunting in the nude, this book is one of the best on the subject.

And, if you want some knock-your-socks-off wild game cookin', look no further.

Professor Phil Hey
Briar Cliff College
Sioux City, Iowa

A Definition

Nude hunting will herein be defined as hunting while in the nude, not hunting for nudes.

This is a family publication, after all.

PREFACE

This book provides the reader with information, guidance, and inspiration on the subject of hunting in the nude.

DEDICATED TO

"Cricket" the cat
who finds
nude hunting
...just alright,
thank you.

Chapter I

WHY?

The "How-tos" and other such considerations about the whole issue of nude hunting are certainly of interest, of course.

But, before we delve into such things we need to ask ourselves "Why?".

It's basically quite simple. I would ask you to think about

the world's best hunters. Some would grant that distinction to the big cats. Those beautiful felines of the jungle are wonderful beasts, indeed.

Others would credit those clever little spiders or maybe birds of prey as being the world's best.

While I choose not to participate in a debate of which among those are the most skillful and effective hunters, I would point out an interesting fact.

**Without exception, every one
of these superb hunters do
their hunting in the nude.**

I'm not going to get all bogged down in any semantics about the role of hair or feathers. The bottom line is that these industrial strength hunters just flat out don't wear any clothes.

Since all these critters do hunt very well, and do so in the nude, it becomes abundantly clear that there is more than simply a casual relationship between hunting skills and ~~nudeity~~ ~~nuditty~~ ... ~~nudee~~ ... ~~nudiety~~ ... going without any clothes.

Since the effectiveness of a hunter is of great importance, the fact that the world's best hunters do so in their birthday suits is sufficient cause for us to follow their lead.

Antelope

Antelope or Venison

4-6 servings or round roast or
steak (strips)
½ tsp. chili powder & Accent
2 T. butter

1½ onion (chopped)
1 can beef broth or beef bouillon
1 can golden mushroom soup
1 (4 oz.) can mushrooms

Sprinkle meat strips with Accent and chili powder. Roll in flour and brown in grease. Remove meat from skillet and drain off grease. Put butter and onion in skillet and brown. Add 2 or 3 T. flour for thickening. Stir until browned lightly. Put in beef broth soup and mushrooms. When well blended, put meat back in and simmer on low at least 1 hour, longer if you can. Add red cooking wine to sauce for fuller flavor. Serve with cooked rice or potatoes.

Antelope What's Been Braised

4 lbs. antelope
4 strips salt pork
Salt & pepper, to taste
1/8 tsp. cinnamon
1/8 tsp. cloves
⅔ C. claret or weak vinegar

½ C. water
1 bay leaf
½ onion (sliced thin)
1 C. claret or cranberry juice
1 C. milk

Trim off all fat and rub with lard or salt pork. Season with salt and pepper, cinnamon, and cloves. Marinate in claret or vinegar for 2 to 3 days in a cold place. Drain and place in baking pan; add water, cover, and cook in slow oven (300°) about 1 hour. Add bay leaf, onion, claret or cranberry juice; cover and cook until tender, about 1 hour. Remove meat and add milk to drippings. Add 1 T. of flour and stir. Heat to boiling and serve with the antelope. Serve garnished with spiced apple rings.

Bear

Stewed Bear

8 lb. bear meat
4 bags carrots
1 bag onions (No. 3 size)
1 stalk celery

1 jigger (1½ oz.) vinegar
4 (8 oz. ea.) cans mushrooms
Dash of garlic salt
Salt & pepper

Cut all fat from meat, cube meat into large pieces, and brown. Clean and cube all vegetables and simmer meat with half of the cleaned carrots, half of the onions, all of the celery, and the jigger of vinegar. When meat and vegetables are cooked, remove carrots, celery, and onions; discard. Put in remaining carrots and onions; simmer again. Cook until done and add mushrooms. Thicken stew as you would gravy. Season with salt, pepper, and garlic salt, to taste. Serves 12.

Flat Out Good Marinated Bear Steak

Thick slice of bear loin
 (cut into steaks)
1 onion (chopped fine)
1 carrot (diced)
1 tsp. paprika
1 C. cider
1 T. lemon juice
1 clove of garlic (crushed)
1 bay leaf
¼ tsp. nutmeg

½ tsp. dry mustard
2 T. orange juice
1 clove garlic (crushed)
4 T. butter
1 tsp. prepared mustard
¼ tsp. Worcestershire sauce
½ tsp. salt
1/8 tsp. pepper
½ tsp. paprika
2 T. tomato juice

Combine the first 11 ingredients, except the meat and bring slowly to a boil. Boil for 5 minutes, then cool. Use to marinate bear steaks 24 hours in refrigerator. Remove steaks from marinade and sear on both sides in broiler under high heat. Reduce heat and broil, basting often with a mixture of the last 8 ingredients. When steaks are done, dust with salt, pepper, and parsley. Serve with mushrooms, sauteed in butter.

Cabbage/Bear Rolls

12 large cabbage leaves
1½ lbs. ground bear meat
 or shredded venison
1 beaten egg
½ C. milk
¼ C. finely chopped onion
1 tsp. Worcestershire sauce
Ground pepper

1½ C. cooked rice
1 (10¾ oz.) can condensed
 tomato soup
1 T. brown sugar
1 T. lemon juice
2 T. chopped dill
1 T. garlic salt

In mixing bowl combine egg, milk, onion, Worcestershire sauce, pepper, garlic, and salt; mix well. Add ground meat and cooked rice; mix thoroughly. Immerse leaves in boiling water until limp, about 3 minutes; drain. Place ⅓ C. meat mixture on each large leaf; fold in sides. Starting at bottom of leaf, roll-up each leaf making sure folded sides are included in roll. Arrange in a 12x7½x2-inch baking pan. Stir together condensed tomato soup, brown sugar, dill, and lemon juice; pour sauce mixture over cabbage rolls. Bake, uncovered at 350° for 1¼ hours, basting once or twice with sauce. Serves 6.

Coon

Coon What's Been Baked

1 tender adult raccoon
4 large apples
2 medium onions (chopped)
3-4 T. butter

3-4 C. dry bread cubes
Sage, to taste
Salt
Pepper

Clean fresh coon and soak in strong salt water overnight or 1 whole day. When ready to prepare remove from water and dry thoroughly with towel. Fill cavity with mixture of seasoned bread, diced apples, and chopped onion. Butter outside meat and sprinkle with seasoning. Bake at 350° in open roaster for approximately 20 minutes per pound or until done. Discard filling and serve with applesauce.

Rackety Coon Sloppy Joes

1 raccoon
1 onion (chopped)
1 green pepper (chopped)
2 stalks celery (chopped)

1 can chopped mushrooms
1 C. barbecue sauce
1 tsp. Lawry's seasoning salt
Dash of pepper

Trim fat from raccoon, cut into large pieces. Pressure cook or boil in water until meat falls off bones. Drain and break meat up into heavy cooking pan. Add other ingredients and simmer approximately ½ hour, stirring occasionally. Add more barbecue sauce if needed. Serve on hamburger buns or homemade biscuits.

Raccoon, BBQ-ed

4-5 lbs. raccoon (halved)
Water to cover
1½ T. salt
1 tsp. pepper

1 medium onion (chopped)
1 T. vinegar
18 oz. bottle BBQ sauce

In Dutch oven, precook raccoon in water for 1½ hours; drain well. Discard liquid and return meat to oven. Add seasoning and onion. Cover and cook over low heat, adding water to keep meat from sticking, 1 hour. Combine vinegar and BBQ sauce. Drain liquid from meat. Spoon sauce over meat and continue cooking 1-1½ hours or until meat is fork tender.

Coon Roasted with Veggies

Clean and remove scent glands from coon as directed. Soak coon and rinse and dry. Score meat and press slices of onion into splits. Roll coon pieces, best cut in serving pieces or whole in flour that the following has been added:

1 C. flour
1 tsp. salt
1½ tsp. paprika

½ tsp. curry powder
¼ tsp. pepper
Vegetables as shown below

Brown raccoon in oil. Put in roasting pan; with drippings that 1½ C. water has been added. Grind 1 green pepper and 2 carrots; spread this on raccoon. Bake at 350° for 45 minutes, covered. Meanwhile, prepare 6 medium white potatoes, 3 small sweet potatoes, 6 carrots, 3 stalks celery (cubed), 3 apples (peeled and halved), onions may be added. Arrange around coon and bake an additional 30 minutes, covered and cook until tender. Serves 6 to 8.

Coon, Fricasseed

1 raccoon
¾ C. flour
1 tsp. paprika

1½ tsp. salt
¼ tsp. black pepper
3 T. oil or bacon drippings

Clean raccoon as directed and soak in solution of soda and water; rinse and dry. Cut in serving pieces. Dredge raccoon pieces in flour that has paprika, salt, and pepper added. Brown in oil. Place in roaster. Add 2 C. water; cover and simmer until tender. For variety, add 2 onions (sliced thin), added to the last 30 minutes or roasting, gives a delicious flavor. Variety II: Add sliced sweet potatoes to the last 30 minutes of roasting, gives raccoon a tang. Sprinkle with juice of 1 lemon the last 10 minutes of roasting or until sweet potatoes are tender.

Duck

Apple 'N Roast Duck

2 large Mallard ducks
½ C. chopped celery
½ C. chopped onion
2 medium apples (cut-up)
¼ C. brown sugar
¼ C. chopped walnuts
2 to 4 slices bread (cubed)

¼ C. raisins
Dash of pepper
½ tsp. salt
1/8 tsp. marjoram
Dash of sage
1 bouillon cube
1 C. warm water

Soak ducks overnight in salt and water brine. Drain and place in roasting pan. Mix celery, onion, apples, brown sugar, walnuts, bread cubes, raisins and seasonings. Dissolve bouillon cube in 1 cup warm water; add ½ C. bouillon to dressing mixture to moisten. Place dressing around ducks. Pour remaining bouillon over ducks. Bake at 325° for 1 hour and 30 minutes or until done. Serves 4.

Sausage 'N Duck

STUFFING:
½ lb. unseasoned pork sausage
¼ C. grated onion
½ C. fine-cut celery
1 T. minced parsley
2 T. grated green pepper
1½ C. cold water

½ tsp. pepper
1 tsp. salt
4 C. dry bread cubes
½ tsp. sage or poultry seasoning
¼ C. melted butter

Mix well the first 8 ingredients and cook for 40 to 45 minutes. Remove from heat and cool until grease sets. Remove as much of the grease as possible. Add bread cubes, sage or poultry seasoning, and melted butter. Toss to mix well, adding more moisture if necessary, milk or water.

To Prepare Duck: Rub inside of duck lightly with salt. Put stuffing lightly into cavity and skewer or lace opening. Brush outside with soft shortening and dust with flour. Place in covered roasting pan, breast side up and roast in 325° oven for 3½ to 4 hours or until breast meat starts to fall off bone. Baste at 45 minutes intervals, and season with salt and pepper. Serves 2.

Slightly Wonderful Duck

5 Jonathan apples
Bacon strips
Ducks (2 Mallards)

1 C. raisins
Salt and pepper
Spices

Season ducks with salt and pepper inside and out. Don't peel apple, quarter them, and place some apples and some raisins in each duck. Place ducks in roasting pan and put the rest of the apples and raisins around them. Add the spices which you favor. Place bacon strips on each duck. Pour about 1½ C. of water into the pan. Bake at 350° until tender. Add more water, if needed.

Bluebills, Special

6 bluebills
10 ozs. Italian dressing

1 onion
8 hamburger buns

Fillet out breasts of ducks by peeling back skin and taking meat only. Soak fillets in dressing overnight after beating each with tenderizer (pope hammer). Remove from marinade, salt, and pepper; barbecue over charcoal 4 minutes on a side. Serve on buttered buns with slice of onion. Be sure to not overcook. Makes a great lunch on a duck hunt. Can easily be carried to the blind. Serves 4.

Chapter II

COLORS & SAFETY

I think that most of our dear readers would agree that hunters dressed up the earlier traditional earth toned colors would often resemble a game animal. A careless hunter with deer-colored clothes on could

find himself pitched in the back of a pick up truck with his tongue hanging out and with a little bitty paper tag around his ankle.

With the wrong clothes on, a hunter can look distress-ingly like a pheasant, a rabbit, or even a squirrel to a trigger-happy hunter who has spent so many hours behind a desk that he's got his brains addled.

Yes, it's the browns, greens, and other earth tones that folks have tended to wear in the woods that's done a lot of 'em in.

An alternative, of course, is to wear the bright orange instead of those offending colors. That has been the tradition of recent times, of course.

Another strategy, of course, is to wear your birthday suit, and present the color of skin to the world. To do that would make the orange color quite irrelevant.

The only time an in-the-nude hunter would have occasion to be concerned would be when he was in the company of game animals that looked like himself.

However, it doesn't take a whole lot of study before one comes to the realization that there really aren't a great number of critters that look like a stark naked human being. There is, for example almost no similarity in appearance between a prairie chicken (see left) and a human bean.

One critter that does, however, look like a human is a freshly shaven kangaroo.

Newly shaven kangaroos have a striking similarity to human beans.

Therefore, a little judicious avoidance of associating with freshly shaven kangaroos during hunting season would be well advised for hunters who happen to be doing their thing in the nude.

Fish

Fish in a Pickle

7 lbs. fish filets
1 qt. granulated sugar
3 qts. white vinegar

1¾ C. salt
1 box pickling spice
2 medium onions (sliced)

Mix fish and salt in glass container (1 gallon jar works well). Cover with vinegar. Soak for 5 days in refrigerator. Drain and soak in cold water for 1 hour. Wash well and dry. Mix 2 qts. white vinegar, 1 qt. granulated sugar, and 1 box (5 ozs.) pickling spices and heat until sugar is dissolved. Arrange fish and onion slice in 1 gallon jar. Cover with cool solution. Refrigerate for another 5 days.

Smokey Fish

BRINE:
1 gallon water
4 C. salt
2 C. brown sugar

2 T. crushed black pepper
2 T. crushed bay leaves

Soak fish 2 to 3 hours, depending on size in brine. Remove from brine and rinse with fresh water. Hang in cool shady place for 3 hours or until shiny skin forms on fish. Place in smoker for 4 hours at 110°-120°. Then add dense smoke and raise temperature to 160°-180° for 4 hours.

Some More Fish in a Pickle

2 lbs. cut-up fish fillets

2 C. water

½ C. canning salt

Cover and let stand in refrigerator for 24 hours. Pour off above liquid. Soak in distilled white vinegar for 24 hours. Pour off above liquid. Cut and chop lots of onion and alternate with packing of fish in jars. Then boil the following mixture:

1 C. white vinegar

1½ C. sugar

½ C. water

2-3 tsp. pickling spice

Boil and set aside to cool. Then add ½ C. port white wine. Put 10 to 15 whole allspice on top of fish, then pour above liquid mixture over fish. (I usually add a bay leaf to each jar, optional.) Put lids on and keep refrigerated.

Carp in a Can

Carp

Vegetable oil

Ketchup

Salt

Vinegar

Clean fish and cut into chunks. Pack fish into pint jars. Leave at least 1-inch from top of jar. To each pint add 2 T. each of ketchup, vinegar, and oil plus 1 tsp. salt. Seal jars and put in pressure canner at 10 lbs. of pressure for 80 minutes. Bones become soft and fish has salmon taste.

More Canned Fish

Per pint cut up fish in 2-inch squares and pack in jars.

ADD:
½ tsp. canning salt   3 T. vinegar

Seal and put in pressure cooker for 75 minutes on 10 lbs. pressure. DON'T add any extra water (it will make its own juice). Cool cooker before removing jars.

Trout Filets or Steak

2 lbs. trout filets   2 T. lemon juice
  or steaks   1 tsp. grated onion
Salt and pepper   ¼ C. butter or margarine (melted)

Heat oven to 350°. If filets are large, cut into serving pieces. Season with salt and pepper. Mix juice, onion, and butter. Dip fish into butter mixture. Place in greased 9x9x2-inch pan. Pour remaining butter mixture over fish. Bake, uncovered for 25 to 30 minutes until fish flakes easily with a fork.

Hot Dish Pike

1 Northern Pike fillets
1 small can diced mushrooms
1 can drained bean sprouts
4 ozs. peas

1 C. skim milk
Salt, pepper & paprika
Mozzarella cheese

Cut fillets into small pieces. Add ingredients in casserole dish and mix together. Sprinkle salt and pepper, to taste. Add mozzarella cheese on top. Sprinkle lightly with paprika after baking for 1 hour at 350°.

Broasted Trout

4 medium pan-sized trout
4-5 slices white bread
4 slices bacon
  (cut into ½-inch pieces)
1 medium onion
  (half chopped, half sliced)
½ tsp. pepper

1 can mushroom slices (drained)
1 large lemon
1 celery rib (chopped fine,
  leaves and all)
½ tsp. savory
½ tsp. salt

Clean, wash, and pat dry the fish, leaving heads and tails on. Fry the bacon until nearly crisp; remove and set aside. Drain off all but about 2 T. of grease. Cook the chopped onion and celery in the bacon drippings until soft but not browned; remove and add to the bacon. Cut bread into cubes and fry in the bacon grease until lightly browned. Remove pan from the flame and add mushrooms, bacon, onions, and celery. Toss lightly with two forks; sprinkle with salt, pepper, and savory; toss again. Stuff trout loosely with this mixture. Prepare two large layered rectangles of aluminum foil. Place thin slices of onion on foil with two trout on top head to tail. Sprinkle with lemon   juice. Fold foil over and seal edges with double fold. Place in a medium-hot oven, 350°-375° and bake for 20 to 25 minutes. Open foil and test for doneness; you may want to cook another 5 to 10 minutes.

Piggy Bass, Baked

6 medium-sized bass
½ C. cornmeal
1½ tsp. salt

1½ tsp. paprika
6 bacon slices

Clean bass and cut into serving pieces. Mix together cornmeal, salt, and paprika. Dip fish in cornmeal mixture. Place in baking dish. Top with bacon. Bake at 425° for about 20 minutes.

Dirt Cheap "Lobster"

2 qts. water
¼-⅓ C. salt
¼ C. vinegar
2 T. dried onion flakes

2 T. dried parsley flakes
1 bay leaf
6-7 large fillets (such as
    walleye, northern, bass, etc.)

Bring water, salt, and vinegar to boil. Add spices and fish. Bring to boil again. Cook until fish are done (about 8 to 10 minutes). Remove from water and put under broiler until dry and crisp (about 3 minutes). Serve with melted butter.

Baked Fish

1 whole large snapper or rockfish
Juice of 7 lemons
Water
Dash of hot pepper sauce
2 onions (sliced)

3 tomatoes (sliced)
2 T. butter or margarine
2 T. oil
1¾ C. dry white wine

Place fish in a shallow baking dish and add lemon juice and enough water to cover fish. Sprinkle with hot pepper sauce, cover, and marinate in refrigerator from 2 to 6 hours. Drain marinade, reserving 1 C. of the liquid. Place onions and tomatoes in baking dish and then the fish, dotting with butter and some oil. Add the saved marinade and wine and bake for 30 to 40 minutes at 350°.

Super Catfish Chowder

5-6 lbs. catfish (skinned & clean)
5-7 potatoes
  (medium, peeled & diced)
1 qt. peeled tomatoes
4 oz. can tomato sauce
1 large onion (chopped)

⅓ lb. butter
½ tsp. thyme
2 T. Worcestershire sauce
Salt (optional)
Pepper, to taste

Place fish in large cook pot and cover with water. Bring to boil. Reduce heat and simmer until fish is well done and flakes. Drain fish, saving liquid, and return it to the pot. Remove bones from fish and return to liquid. Add other ingredients. Cook on low heat to simmer for 1 hour, stirring frequently. Serve hot and enjoy!

Ozark Catfish Balls

Bake or steam catfish. (Modern method is to cook in a pressure cooker.) Remove fish from bones and flake. To every 2 C. flaked fish add 2 T. mashed potatoes, 1 egg, salt, and pepper, to taste. Shape in balls and fry in deep fat.

Super Catfish Soup

2 to 3 lbs. catfish (cut-up)
2 qts. cold water
1 sliced onion
1 chopped celery stalk

Herbs (bay leaf, parsley, thyme)
Salt and pepper
1 C. milk
2 T. butter or fat

Place all ingredients into stew pan and put on slow fire. Stir occasionally and cook until fish is ready to fall to pieces. Serve hot.

Jus' Plain Fried Fish

Scale and clean fish well, and wash very good in cold water. If small, fry them as is. If large, cross-slit them along side so they cook better. Salt them and then roll in flour and meal mixed equally. Fry in ½ to 1-inch of hot fat. Turn and brown on both sides. Serve hot.

Better Batter ala Fish

¼ C. cornstarch
¼ C. beer
2 eggs (separated)

¼ C. flour
Pinch of salt
Pinch of sugar

Mix beer in egg yolks and add the rest of the ingredients. Beat egg whites until stiff. Fold stiffly beaten egg whites into the egg yolk mixture. Dip fish into this batter and fry until golden brown.

Pheasant

Mom's Pheasant

2 pheasants (cut-up)
Flour
Oil

Salt and pepper
Water

Flour all pieces. Brown in oil in frying pan. Place browned pieces in roaster. Salt and pepper. Add enough water to cover the bottom of pan. Cover and bake at 350° for 1 hour or until done.

Square Pheasant

Filet of pheasant breasts
 from 2 pheasants
1 C. flour
1 tsp. baking powder

½ tsp. salt
1 egg
1 C. milk
¼ C. salad oil

Cut pheasant breasts into 1-inch square pieces. Mix remaining ingredients to form batter. Beat until smooth. Dip pieces into batter and deep fat fry until golden brown. Salt and serve. Serves family of 4.

Pheasant 'N Mushroom

1 dressed pheasant
1 can Campbell's Golden
 Mushroom soup

¼ C. water

Place pheasant, soup, and water in crock pot. Cook on High for 4 hours or Low for 6 hours. Carefully remove all bones from meat and sauce. Great when served with bread and mashed potatoes. Serves family of 4.

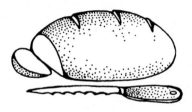

Chapter III

CONTENTIOUS VOICES

Contentious voices have been raised to argue against hunting in the buff.

One of the criticisms of this most natural of all hunting methods is that we have learned, so long ago, to judge people's character by their clothes.

This analytical method of determining the nature of people bears on such things as the person's social standing, level of affluence, and gender. We all know that boys dress differently than girls. Even in the field, while hunting, there are distinctive differences in attire between boys and girls.

This criticism of hunting in the nude says that if hunters were running around au naturel, we wouldn't be able to tell the boys from the girls.

Without such helpful hints such as blouses, light shoes or heavy boots, decorative trim, and so forth, we'd be all but at a loss as to being able to tell if a buck naked hunter we'd stumble across in the field was a boy or a girl.

This situation, these folks will claim, would be not nearly as good as more traditional situations where folks wear clothes.

The author proposed that such criticism is quite beside the point. Serious hunters are serious hunters and when they are out there in the field, they really have no reason to concern themselves with each other's gender. You know what they say about gasoline and alcohol. Well, just the about same thing is true of gunpowder and perfume.

Another criticism of hunting in the nude is that it would prevent one's wearing of the protective orange.

We are not proposing the abandonment of safety procedures at all, of course. On the contrary, we are quite concerned about them. So there!!

Pleasant Pheasant Casserole

2 beaten eggs
2 C. broth (from cooking pheasant)
1 can mushroom soup
½ C. chopped onion
¼ tsp. salt

¾ C. chopped celery
¾ C. grated American cheese
2½ C. crushed Ritz crackers
Boned pheasant
¼ tsp. pepper

Cook 1 pheasant in salt water until tender. Save broth. Mix all ingredients, turn into buttered baking dish and bake at 350° for 1 hour.

Aunt Hattie's Pheasant

1 pheasant
½ C. butter
1 T. dried chives
1 tsp. rosemary
1 T. parsley flakes
½ C. orange juice (undiluted)

½ C. white wine
1 C. water
1 C. rice (regular, not minute)
Salt and pepper
1 orange (sliced in rounds)

Quarter pheasant, place in large skillet and brown in butter. Add chives, salt, pepper, and remaining spices. Add juice, wine, and water. Cover and cook over low heat for ½ hour. Add rice, cover, and cook for ½ hour. About 5 minutes before serving, add orange slices and cover to warm. Serves 2.

Super Pheasant

2 pheasants
1 (3 oz.) can mushrooms
1 T. grated cheese
2 C. uncooked rice
2 tsp. chicken seasoned
   stock base

1 C. chopped parsley
2 C. water
½ stick butter
2 T. oil
3 T. flour
Salt and pepper

Dredge pheasant parts in flour; saute' in 2 T. oil until just browned. Mix mushrooms, uncooked rice, cheese, soup base, water, parsley, salt, and pepper. Pour into greased roaster or casserole. Arrange pheasant on top. Bake, covered in 325° oven for 2 hours.

Pheasant in Batter

2 eggs

2 T. water

MIX:
½ C. flour
2 slices dried bread (crumbs)
Cooking oil

1 can mushroom soup
½ can water

   Beat eggs and water; refrigerate for an hour. Should be gooey. Dip pheasant pieces into egg batter and roll in flour, dip again and roll in crumbs. Refrigerate for 2 hours. Heat ½-inch cooking oil and brown pieces on both sides. Salt pieces and place in casserole dish. Pour mushroom soup over pheasant. Cover tightly and bake at 350° for an hour.

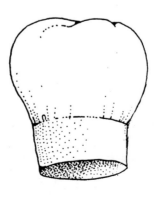

Ricey Pheasant

Cut-up pheasant
1 can cream of celery soup
1 can cream of mushroom soup
1 can milk (use soup can to measure)

1 pkg. Lipton's dry onion soup
1 pkg. Uncle Ben's wild &
long grain rice

Mix all ingredients together, except pheasant. Pour mixture into 9x13-inch baking dish. Lay pheasant on top and cover with foil. Bake at 325° for 2 hours. Uncover the last half hour.

Roast Pheasant 'N Sherry

1 pheasant
1 small bay leaf
1 clove garlic
Few celery leaves
1 slice lemon

3-4 slices bacon
1 C. chicken broth
2 T. flour
3 T. dry sherry

Season inside of bird with salt. Stuff with bay leaf, garlic clove, celery leaves, lemon, and bacon slices; truss. Roast pheasant at 325° for 2 hours or until tender. Remove string and discard stuffing. Serve on bed of rice and accompany with Sherry Sauce.

Pheasant with Better Batter

2 eggs

2 T. water

MIX:
½ C. flour
2 slices dried bread (crumbs)
Cooking oil

1 can mushroom soup
½ can water

Beat eggs and water; refrigerate for an hour. Should be gooey. Dip pheasant pieces into egg batter and roll in flour, dip again, and roll in crumbs. Refrigerate for 2 hours. Heat ½-inch cooking oil and brown pieces on both sides. Salt pieces and place in casserole dish. Pour mushroom soup over pheasant. Cover tightly and bake at 350° for an hour.

Pheasant 'N Wild Rice

1 can mushrooms & juice
1 box Uncle Ben's long
   grain & wild rice

1 can chicken broth
1 pheasant (cut-up or whole)
Mrs. Dash

In a 9x13-inch pan put rice, mushrooms, mushroom juice, and chicken broth. Mix well. Lay pheasant (it's easier cut-up) on top and sprinkle with Mrs. Dash. Bake at 350 for 1 hour.

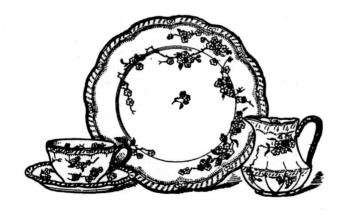

Jus' Plain Roast Pheasant

Dressed pheasant
Salt and pepper
Butter

Apples (sliced)
Bacon strips

Stuffed dressed pheasant with apples and season with salt and pepper. Cover breast with thin strips of bacon.

A fine young pheasant should be roasted at 350° about 45 minutes to 1 hour, and be generously basted with butter.

And More Jus' Plain Roast Pheasant

Pheasant (cut-up)
1 can cream of chicken soup
1 can cream of mushroom soup
1 can sherry
2 T. snipped pimiento
1 can mushrooms (drained)

Salt
Pepper
Poultry seasoning
Curry powder
1-1½ sticks margarine
Slivered almonds

Dredge pheasant in flour and brown in frying pan in 1-1½ sticks melted margarine. Season liberally with salt, pepper, poultry seasonings, and curry powder. Place in 9x12-inch pan and pour rest of mixed ingredients over it. Sprinkle top with slivered almonds, cover tightly with foil. Bake at 300° for 4 hours.

Smothered Pheasant

1 pheasant (cleaned)
½ C. flour
¼ tsp. poultry seasoning
½ tsp. salt

¼ tsp. pepper
½ C. cooking oil
1 C. milk or light cream

Cut pheasant into serving pieces. Combine flour and seasonings in a paper bag. Heat oil over medium heat in a large skillet. Shake pheasant in bag. Place in skillet to brown. Add milk and cover. Cook over low heat until done, about 1 hour.

Mc'Pheasants

6 lbs. pheasant or turkey
  (raw, ground)
2 lbs. pork sausage
Flour

Salt, pepper and poultry
  seasoning, to taste
2 eggs (beaten)
Rolled cracker crumbs

Mix poultry meat, sausage, salt, pepper, and poultry seasoning. Form into patties. Roll patties in flour, dip in egg, and roll in cracker crumbs. Brown in skillet and finish in 325° oven for 1¾ hours. Add water as needed or add 1 can cream of mushroom soup.

Chapter IV

REASONABLE SEASONABLES

A significant element of this whole business of nude hunting is, of course, the array of environmental factors that we are subject to. Chief among these are cold and thorns.

The thorn problem is one that doesn't lend itself to a whole lot of fixin', but the temperature problem can be significantly reduced by adjustments in the hunting seasons set by law.

For example, if a season is normally from Dec. 1 through Feb. 1, there will be few days during that sixty-one day period when the nude hunter can do his or her thing. That is simply because of the cold weather during those two months right there in the dead of winter.

Well, what we deserve is a sixty-one day crack at hunting just like the folks that go out into the woods fully clad. A hunting season consisting of sixty-one days of decent weather would be a reasonable alternative to the rigidity of certain prescribed days. For instance, the interests of nude hunters would be well served if one had the first sixty-one days in which the termperature got above 60 degrees. That would be far better than the December first through February first scheme.

You can help further this idea by supporting our political action committee BURR (Brotherhood for Undertaking Reasonable Regulations).

It would be convenient if your contribution to BURR was in some multiple of the cost of a good pizza (with thin crust) and iced tea.

Please send your contributions to Irma Biggs, Chief Creative Accountant, Quixote Press, Wever, IA.

Phancy Pheasant

3 hard-cooked eggs (chopped)
4 C. cooked pheasant (chopped)
3 C. crackers (crumbled)
1 C. grated aged cheese
1 can green asparagus
½ C. melted butter

2 C. milk, plus asparagus juice
3 T. flour
Salt and pepper, to taste
½ tsp. grated lemon rind
1 can red pimientos (chopped)
1 T. butter

Melt butter, blend in flour, salt and pepper, lemon rind, stirring constantly and cook until thick. Add eggs, cheese, and pimientos. Saute' crackers in butter. In a 2-quart casserole, layer white sauce, pheasant crumbs; ending up with crumbs. Bake at 350° for 20 to 30 minutes until brown on top. Serves 6 to 8. May be baked in a 9x13-inch dish.

Braised Pheasant in Sour Cream

1 dressed pheasant
3 T. flour
1½ tsp. salt
3 T. butter
1½ C. water

¼ tsp. sugar
½ tsp. paprika
1 C. sour cream
Onion, if desired

Clean pheasant. Be sure to remove pin feathers. Rinse well and drain. Cut into serving pieces. Dredge in flour, salt, and pepper. Brown slowly on all sides in butter. Blend only remaining flour into butter in the pan. Add ¼-½ C. water and blend until smooth. Lower heat, cover, and simmer for 1¾ hours or until tender. Adding remaining water as needed. Add remaining ingredients and blend well. Simmer gently for 15 minutes. Simmer onions for the full cooking time.

Creamy Pheasant

1 pheasant, dressed
⅓ C. flour
1 C. water
1 tsp. salt
¼ tsp. black pepper

¼ C. oil or margarine
1 C. cream
1 tsp. minced onion
Pinch of thyme

Clean and remove pin feathers, singe pheasant. Soak in solution of 2 qts. water, 1 T. salt, and 1 tsp. vinegar. Rinse thoroughly and drain; cut into serving pieces. Dredge in flour, salt, and pepper. Brown slowly on all sides in oil or margarine, about 10 to 15 minutes. Blend in any remaining flour and thyme in oil in pan. Add water and simmer for 1 hour, covered. Add onion and cream and simmer until tender. Serve with boiled potatoes with jackets on. Serves 4 to 5. Garnish with paprika and parsley.

Note: For sour pheasant, substitute sour cream for sweet cream, dill weed for thyme, and add ¼ to ½ tsp. sugar.

Dumpled Pheasant

1 pheasant (cut-up)
1 can mushroom soup
1 soup can milk

1 large sliced onion
¼ C. white wine

Roll cut-up pheasant in seasoned flour, and brown; put in roaster. Mix mushroom soup, milk, and pour over pheasant. Slice onion and lay over pheasant, then pour over wine. Cover and bake at 300° for 3 hours or until tender. Always moist, this can be used for all small wild game.

Super Pheasant

Pheasant
1 can (small) orange juice
¼ C. brown sugar

¼ tsp. ginger
Salt & pepper

Shake pheasant pieces in flour and brown in butter. Place in baking pan. Mix orange juice with brown sugar and ginger; pour over pheasant. Season with salt and pepper. Bake until tender.

Quail

Fried Quail

Cut-up quail as desired. (It is usually best to have three pieces — breast and two legs. (Season with salt and pepper; roll pieces in flour. Place in hot deep fat and brown quickly on both sides. Turn down heat and cover pan; let cook slowly until tender. Make gravy right in the same skillet using residue left from frying.

Quail and Wild Rice

5-6 quail
6 oz. pkg. Uncle Ben's long
  grain & wild rice
⅓ C. onion (chopped)
¼ C. margarine

⅓ C. flour
1 tsp. salt
Dash of pepper
1 C. Half 'N Half or whole milk
1 C. quail broth

Stew quail until tender, about 1 hour. Remove meat from bones. Cook rice according to package directions, using foil packet of seasonings. Saute' onion and green pepper in margarine. Add flour, salt, and pepper; stir to blend. Gradually stir in cream and broth. Cook until thickened. Mix all and put in a greased 2-quart casserole. Bake at 350° for about 1 hour.

Braggin' Time Roast Quail

Make a rich biscuit dough, using milk or cream for mixing. Roll thin; spread with butter, fold, and roll again. Line a baking pan with the dough. Split dressed quail down the back, lay them in the pan and sprinkle with salt and pepper; spread each bird with butter. Add boiling water, about ⅔ C. to each bird. Cover with crust and make some small slits to let out steam, and bake in medium oven until done.

Roast Quail

4 dressed quail
6 T. butter
Salt
Pepper
3 T. cognac

1 C. chicken stock
1-2 tsp. lemon juice
30 white grapes (halved & seeded)
2 apples (sliced)
¼ C. vermouth

Rub quail generously with butter, salt, and pepper. Put a lump of butter, ½ of apple (sliced) or 4 white grapes in cavities. Sprinkle with cognac. Roast at 400° for 15 minutes, basting every 5 minutes. While quail are roasting, gently heat seeded and halved grapes in vermouth and chicken stock. Remove grapes and add these to quail; roast another 15 minutes. Remove quail to heated serving platter. Add the vermouth and chicken stock to pan juices with lemon juice. Stir well. Pour sauce over quail. Garnish and serve.

Tipsy Quail

2 small onions
½ C. fat
1 tsp. peppercorns
2 whole cloves
2 cloves garlic (cut fine)
6 quail
½ bay leaf

2 C. white wine
1/8 tsp. pepper
½ tsp. salt
1 tsp. minced chives
Few grains cayenne
2 C. cream of evaporated milk

Melt fat; add cloves, peppercorns, garlic, bay leaf, and onions. Cook for several minutes. Add quail and brown. Add salt and pepper, cayenne, wine, and chives. Simmer for about 40 minutes. Remove quail; strain sauce and add cream and heat to boiling point. Pour over quail. Serves 2.

Baked Tipsy Quail

6 quail
½ C. fat
2 small onions
2 whole cloves
2 cloves garlic

½ bay leaf
2 C. wine
½ tsp. salt
¼ tsp. pepper
2 C. cream or evaporated milk

Brown birds in fat, onions, cloves, garlic, and bay leaf. Cook several minutes. Add wine, salt, and pepper; simmer until tender, about 30 minutes. Remove quail; strain sauce. Add cream and heat to boiling; pour over quail.

49

Rabbit

Dumpled Rabbit

2 rabbits
1 or 2 bay leaves (optional)
½ tsp. garlic powder
   (optional)

1 large or 2 small onions
   (cut in large pieces)
Salt and pepper, to taste

Put rabbit in kettle, almost covered with water. Add seasonings and bring to a boil. Boil slowly until meat is tender, but doesn't fall off bone. Remove meat from broth and thicken with flour or cornstarch to consistency of gravy. Put rabbit in gravy, top with dumplings.

DUMPLINGS:
½ C. milk
2½ tsp. baking powder
¼ tsp. salt

1 to 1½ C. flour
1 medium egg

Mix all together and drop in broth.

French Fried Rabbit

1 rabbit (cut in pieces)
Salt
1 medium onion (sliced)
2 T. flour

½ C. evaporated milk
2 eggs (beaten)
Cracker crumbs

Parboil rabbit for 45 minutes in salted water in which onion has been added. Remove and drain on paper toweling. Mix flour, milk, and eggs. Dip rabbit in egg, then in crumbs. Fry in deep fat until golden.

Rabbit 'N All Kinds of Other Stuff

1 (2½ lb.) rabbit
  (cut in serving pieces)
6 small white onions
1 bay leaf
1½ C. diced celery
4½ tsp. salt
1/8 tsp. pepper

2 qt. boiling water
2 C. diced potatoes
½ lb. fresh mushrooms (sliced)
½ C. flour
½ C. cold water
1 T. snipped parsley
Dash of Tabasco

Wash and dry cleaned rabbit. Place in kettle with onions, bay leaf, celery, salt, pepper, and water. Simmer, covered for 2 hours or until rabbit is nearly tender. Add potatoes, carrots, and mushrooms. Simmer, covered for 30 minutes or until all is tender. Blend flour with water. Stir into stew and cook until thickened. Add parsley and Tabasco sauce. Serves 6.

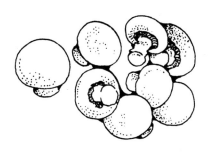

Rabbit Foursome

4 rabbits
1 can mushroom soup
3 C. water

1 tsp. salt
½ tsp. pepper

In a small roaster put in all ingredients and let cook at 350° for about 1 hour.

Rabbit 'N Gravy

Rabbit (cut-up)
Salt
Black pepper
1 tsp. finely chopped garlic
4 T. butter

1 C. flour
4 T. oil
¼ C. chopped onions
1 C. chicken broth
1 C. sour cream

Sprinkle each piece with salt and pepper. Flour each piece thoroughly. Heat butter and oil in heavy skillet. Brown rabbit pieces. Cover and cook on lowest heat until tender. Remove meat to platter or dish. Pour off all but a thin flim of fat. Add chopped onion and garlic. Cook for 3 to 4 minutes. Pour in chicken stock. Boil briskly until stock is reduced by about a third. Turn down heat and with a whisk slowly beat in sour cream. Simmer only long enough to heat gravy through. Pour over rabbit or serve separately.

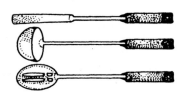

Chapter V

ANIMAL RIGHTISTS

It is really important for the hunter-in-the-buff to be aware of the situation he/she should avoid at all costs.

Never, never, never get drawn into any augument, debate, or discussion about the controversial subject of hunting vs. animal rights.

Anybody, even those fully clothed folks, can work himself into an ulcer arguing with animal rightists. But, if you tackle the job of righteously and indignantly pontificating on the philosophical elements of hunting vs. animal rights while you're in the nude, you're gonna end up looking awfully silly.

Best to just avoid the whole subject.

Jus' Plain Fried Rabbit

2 rabbits (2-3 lbs. ea.)
2 egg yolks (beaten)
3 C. milk
1¼ C. flour

1 tsp. salt
½ C. Crisco
Parsley

Clean dressed rabbits and soak in cold salt water for 2 hours. Cut-up and dry off pieces. Combine egg yolks and 1 C. milk; add 1 C. flour a little at a time. Add salt and beat until smooth. Dip rabbit into batter and fry until brown, 15 to 20 minutes. Reduce heat and continue cooking until tender, 40 to 45 minutes, turning often. Make a gravy by adding remaining flour to the fat in pan. Add the remaining milk gradually, stirring constantly. Bring to boil. Salt and pepper and pour over fried rabbit. Garnish with chopped parsley. Serves 6.

Rabbit in the Oven

1 rabbit (cut into pieces)
1 C. flour
1 T. paprika
1⅓ tsp. salt

¼ C. melted margarine
¼ C. melted shortening
½ C. water
Black pepper

Mix flour and paprika. Roll rabbit in mixture. Salt and pepper. Place in a greased roaster. Pour melted margarine and shortening over rabbit. Cover and bake at 350° for 2 hours. At the end of 45 minutes, turn each piece and add water. Note: After rabbit has been baking 45 minutes, add 1 medium onion (sliced thin) and continue baking until done. For a tangier taste to the rabbit. Serves 4.

Hasenpfeffer

1 rabbit (cut in serving pieces)
½ C. lemon juice
1 C. butter
Bacon
¼ C. water
1 T. vinegar

2 tsp. salt
1 C. onions
1 T. sugar
⅔ C. sour cream
¼ C. red wine (optional)
Flour

Soak rabbit and cut in serving pieces overnight in enough cold water to cover, mixed with ½ C. lemon juice. Use part of butter to grease heavy roasting pan well. Put in the drained rabbit pieces and cut remainder of butter over top. Cover with strips of bacon. Add ¼ C. water, mixed with the vinegar and salt; sprinkle chopped onions over top and bake at 300° for about 2 hours or until tender and nicely browned. Shortly before it is done, caramelize the sugar and add to sauce in pan. Then add sour cream, mixed with the red wine (optional) and thicken the gravy with flour and water. Serve hot with small boiled potatoes. Serves 3 to 4.

More Rabbit 'N Gravy

1 rabbit (cut in serving pieces)
2 T. oil
2 onions (chopped)
2 C. sour cream
  (dairy sour cream)
2 slices lemon

½ tsp. crushed oregano
1 bay leaf
3 T. wine vinegar
½ tsp. sugar
1½ T. flour

Season rabbit with salt. Dredge rabbit in flour. Put rabbit in hot skillet with oil. Brown rabbit and add 2 chopped onions, 2 slices lemon, ½ tsp. crushed oregano, 1 bay leaf, and black pepper, to taste. Add vinegar and let it steam or simmer until tender. Remove rabbit from skillet. Put 1 T. butter in skillet with 1½ T. flour. Mix well and add 2 C. thick sour cream (dairy sour cream). Bring just to boil and season to taste. Remove bay leaf. If too thick, add a little water. Pour over rabbit and serve with boiled potatoes. Serves 5.

Barely Rabbit

1 (2½ lb.) rabbit
1 C. cornmeal
2 tsp. baking powder
1 C. sifted flour

1 egg
1 tsp. salt
1¼ C. milk
Shortening for rabbit

Mix flour, baking powder, cornmeal, and salt. Add milk and egg. Mix until smooth. Dip rabbit and fry until brown.

Rabbit BBQ

Cut up a 3 lb. rabbit, salt, and pepper. Brown floured rabbit in small amount of shortening. Pour off any excess fat. Put in roaster and pour sauce over it.

SAUCE:

1 small onion (chopped)	1/8 tsp. cayenne pepper
2 T. butter or margarine	½ tsp. dry or prepared mustard
2 T. brown sugar	½ tsp. chili powder
2 T. vinegar	1 C. tomato catsup
½ tsp. salt	1 tsp. paprika
2 T. lemon juice	2 tsp. Worcestershire sauce
¼ tsp. black pepper	1¼ C. water

Melt butter; add onion and brown sugar. Add other ingredients and simmer for 20 minutes. Paint rabbit with pastry brush. Cook at 325° for 1 ½ hours.

Rabbit Hot Dish

In bottom of casserole, place small balls of rabbit sausage or ground rabbit meat. Add scant ⅓ C. rice — layer sliced carrots over rice, potatoes over carrots, onions over potatoes. Season with salt as you go. Pour 1 can tomato soup diluted with ½ C. water over casserole. Whole tomatoes can also be used instead of soup. Sprinkle cheese and paprika over top. Bake at 350° for 1½ hours. It's a whole meal in itself.

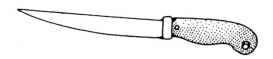

Squirrel

Tater 'N Squirrel

3 small squirrels
  (cut-up in pieces)
½ C. flour
2 T. oil
1 C. water

2 sweet potatoes
  (peeled, cut in halves)
Salt and pepper, to taste
1 T. lemon juice

Dredge squirrel in flour. Salt and pepper, to taste. Brown in hot oil and place browned squirrel in greased roaster. Add water and lemon juice. Bake at 350° for 1¼ hours, basting every 15 minutes. Place sweet potatoes around squirrel and bake 30 more minutes or until squirrel and sweet potatoes are tender. Serves 4 to 5. Note: White potatoes may be used in place of sweet and add 1 C. sliced onions to squirrel the last 30 minutes or roasting.

*"I'm not real sure I want
to do this."*

Chapter VI

LEAVING HOME THE BACON

The experienced nude hunter has learned just real soon in his pursuit of that noble cause, the importance of avoiding another thing.

And, that *this* is bacon. Whatever you do, don't take bacon along with you to cook over the fire.

Let me explain.

We all know about the 4th law of motion and energy in the universe that dictates that a grapefruit squirt will head directly for the eater's eye. A sub-clause of that law also dictates that those itty-bitty little droplets of bacon grease that come out of a fryin' pan at about 67,000,000 degrees Fahrenheit will hone in on the most sensitive spot exposed.

That can be downright terrible, of course. Fact is, that goes beyond terrible to industrial strength awful.

Not cooking bacon while in the nude is a whole lot like not welding while in the nude. The simplest defense is simply not to do bacon at all.

Broiled Squirrel

Place cleaned squirrel on hot broiling rack that has been brushed with butter and sprinkled with salt and pepper. Broil for about 40 minutes, turning frequently and basting with drippings every 10 minutes. Serve with lemon wedges.

Squirrel 'N Mushrooms

3 squirrels, cleaned & cut in serving pieces

¼ C. flour
2 T. oil
1 onion (chopped)
1 can cream of mushroom soup

1 (4 oz.) can mushrooms
½ C. or milk
*   more water may be added)*

Clean and wash squirrels; cover with water that salt and vinegar have been added; soak overnight. Drain and dry. Dredge in seasoned flour and brown in oil. Place in roaster. Mix soup and milk. Sprinkle onion around squirrels. Pour soup mixture over squirrels. Cover and bake at 325° for 1 hour. Add mushrooms and continue baking for 30 minute or until squirrels are tender. Serve with rice or potatoes. Serves 4 to 6.

Squirrel 'N Mushroom Dressing

4 small squirrels
¾ C. cooking oil
¼ C. lemon juice
2 C. bread crumbs
½ C. of Half & Half
4 T. bacon drippings

¼ C. chopped onion
1 (4 oz.) can mushrooms
Salt and pepper, to taste
1 T. chopped parsley
½ C. water

Cover cleaned squirrels with cooking oil that ¼ C. of vinegar has been added; let stand overnight, in cold place (3 to 4 hours if in a hurry). Combine crumbs with the ½ and ½, mushrooms, onions, salt, and pepper. Stuff squirrels with mixture and sew and truss. Brush with bacon drippings. Mix water and lemon juice together; pour around squirrels. Bake at 325° for 1½ to 2 hours, uncovered. Baste every 15 to 20 minutes. Serves 6 to 8.

Roast Squirrels

3 squirrels
¾ C. oil
¼ C. lemon juice
2 C. bread crumbs
½ C. Half & Half

1 C. sauteed mushrooms
½ tsp. salt
¼ tsp. pepper
¼ C. finely chopped onions
4 T. olive oil

Dress and clean squirrels. Soak in cold water about 1 hour. Dry off squirrels. Cover with oil and lemon juice. Let stand for 1 hour. Combine crumbs with just enough milk to moisten, mushrooms, salt, pepper, and onions. Stuff squirrels with this mixture. Put in roaster, brush with olive oil. Roast uncovered at 325° for 1½-2 hours until tender. Baste every 15 minutes. Good served with pan gravy. Serves 6.

More Baked Squirrel

4 squirrels (cut-up)
Flour
1 can bouillon
¼ C. Worcestershire sauce
2 T. chopped parsley

2 T. onion juice
1 clove garlic
1 small bay leaf
Salt and pepper

Dredge squirrels with flour and brown in roasting pan. Add remaining ingredients. Bake at 350° for 45 minutes. Reduce heat and bake slowly until tender. Serves 4 to 6.

Squirrel Fricassee

1 young squirrel (cut in pieces)
½ C. flour
½ tsp. salt
1/8 tsp. pepper

3 slices bacon (cubed)
¼ C. onion (chopped)
10½ oz. can chicken broth

Mix flour, salt, and pepper in bowl. Coat squirrel with mixture. Fry bacon until grease begins to collect. Add meat and fry until well browned. Add onion and broth. Cover and reduce heat to low. Cook for 2 to 2½ hours or until tender. If desired, make gravy from pan drippings just before serving.

Turtle

Stumpy's Snappin' Turtle Stew

2 lbs. prepared turtle meat
Butter
Water for stew
1 medium onion
2 C. celery
1 C. lima beans (soaked)

3 medium potatoes (diced)
1 small can tomatoes
3 medium sized carrots
½ C. chopped parsley
Salt
Pepper

Cut meat in 1-inch pieces. Melt a generous amount of butter in frying pan and brown meat on all sides; remove from heat. Bring water for stew to boil. Add onion, celery, and beans; simmer for ½ hour. Add all ingredients. Cook slowly for 45 minutes.

Turtle Soup

1½ qt. strained chicken broth
1 lb. turtle meat (without bone)
3 T. chicken fat
1 medium onion (chopped)

Salt and pepper, to taste
1 T. chopped parsley
5-6 thin slices lemon

Prepare a richly flavored chicken broth seasoned only with salt; strain. Cut turtle meat into small pieces. Brown slowly in the chicken fat (or butter). Add onion and saute' slowly over medium heat until soft and yellow. Add turtle, seasoning, and any fat to chicken broth; heat to boiling. Reduce heat and simmer gently for 10 minutes. Serve with a sprinkling of parsley on each bowl of soup and a paper-thin slice of lemon floated on top. Serves 5 to 6.

More Turtle Soup

A delicious soup can be prepared the same as with a choice piece of beef or pork. A delicious stew can be made the same by adding the desired vegetables.

Stewed Turtle

3 lbs. turtle meat
4 qts. water
2 onions (chopped)
2 stalks celery (chopped fine)
1 tsp. pickling spices
3 T. butter

1 T. salt
1 tsp. sugar
1 C. tomatoes
½ tsp. black pepper
1 tsp. parsley (chopped)

Place turtle in large kettle with water, salt, and pepper. Tie onion, celery, parsley, and pickling spices in bag and place in kettle with turtle. Bring to a boil and simmer until the turtle meat falls apart. Remove the vegetable and spice bag. Add tomatoes, butter, and sugar. Heat until very hot, and serve.

More Stewed Turtle

2-3 lbs. turtle meat
1 onion (cut-up)
1 tsp. mixed pickling spice
  (tied in bag)
Flour

½ tsp. vinegar
2 tsp. salt
¼ tsp. black pepper
Half & Half

Place turtle in large kettle and cover with water. Add onion, salt, pepper, and the spice bag. Cook turtle until it is tender and falls apart. Remove the turtle from broth, remove spice bag. Thicken the broth with flour like gravy; add about 1 C. of Half & Half or cream may be used, to the soup; add turtle meat and heat just to hot (do not overcook after cream has been added). More vinegar may be added according to taste. Serves 4 to 6.

And Yet Still More Turtle Stew

1 turtle (cut in pieces)
1 large onion (cut-up)
1 tsp. mixed pickling spices
  (tied in bag)

½ tsp. vinegar
3 T. flour
2 C. milk

Combine all ingredients in large kettle, except flour and milk. Fill kettle with as much water as you'll want for soup and enough to cover the turtle. Cover and boil until tender, will take a couple of hours. Pour through a strainer and put juice and meat back in kettle. Take spice bag out after cooking with turtle for 1 hour. Make a thickening of flour and 1 C. of milk. Add to turtle and juice slowly and add rest of milk. Heat but do not boil.

Fried Turtle and Onions

1 turtle (cut in serving pieces)
1 C. flour
3 T. oil
1 tsp. salt

3-4 onions (sliced)
1 clove garlic (crushed) (if desired)
Pepper, to taste
½ tsp. caraway seed

Dredge the turtle in seasoned flour. Fry to brown on all sides in hot oil. Sprinkle with caraway seeds, onion, and garlic. Add 1 C. of water; cover and simmer for 1 hour or until tender and water has cooked away.

Venison

Deer Jerky

1 T. salt
¼ tsp. pepper
3 drops of Tabasco sauce
½ T. garlic salt

¼ T. Worcestershire sauce
Dash of oregano or thyme
1 lb. raw venison
Water

Cut venison into ¼-inch strips. Combine remaining ingredients and pour over meat, adding water, if needed to cover meat. Refrigerate overnight in mixture. Drain meat and pat dry. Bake at 120°-150° for 4 hours.

Chapter VII

TWO BIRDS WITH ONE STREAK

Lots of fellows will head for the woods fully clothed and then shuck all the stuff when they actually get out where they plan on doing their hunting.

But, Ed Felding from near Peoria, Illinois, found a better way.

The better way he found was really all 'cause of his neighbor, Mrs. Swanson. Well, actually, it was Mrs. Swanson's garden that did it all.

You see, Ed, like the other folks in the neighborhood, was an unwilling recipient of Widow Swanson's extra zucchini squash.

You know how that zucchini squash works. If one lousy plant takes a good hold, it will meet the needs of even a large family, with lots left over.

Well, it's those left over ones that ruin perfectly good neighborhoods. Widow Swanson was always foistin' some of those squash off onto Ed.

Ed had tried everything. We'd put a lock on the gate, tried 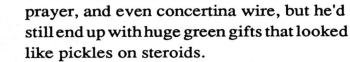 prayer, and even concertina wire, but he'd still end up with huge green gifts that looked like pickles on steroids.

It was hunting in the nude that finally pulled Ed's fat out of the fire. It seemed like the locked gate proved to be only a challenge to the resourcefulness of Widow  Swanson. The prayer seemed to be no more effective, and concertina wire only marginally better.

Almost no matter what Ed would do, just about every morning, he'd find a big sack full of those zucchini squash on his front porch...always with a cute little message from the widow about how she hoped he would enjoy these "couple extra squash" she had ended up with.

Ed's practice of being a nude hunter led him to an effective and permanent answer to the Widow Swanson problem.

Ed's answer was to simply start out from the house in the nude when he went hunting. It was simply a matter of doing that instead of waiting until he got to the woods to do his stripping off.

All he did was to peel everything off, pick up his gear, and amble out the front door right out in front of Widow Swanson and the rest of the world.

Apparently, Widow Swanson was pretty much immune to locks, prayer, and concertina wire, but couldn't quite handle the sight of Ed Felding sans clothes. From the day

that Ed employed that little trick, his porch would be free and clear of any zucchini every morning.

Not only did Ed have the advantage of getting shed of the squash problem, but he was ready to take right off hunting when he hit the field.

That was Ed Felding's solution to the Widow Swanson problem.

Venison in Gravy

1½ lb. ground venison
½ lb. ground pork
1 T. poultry seasoning
1/8 tsp. ground nutmeg
Salt & pepper, to taste

3 T. fat, reserved from browning
3 T. flour
1½ C. cold water
1½ C. cold milk

Mix well together venison, pork, seasonings, and form into patties. Flour outside and brown well in fat; remove to plate. To reserved fat, add flour and mix well, scraping bottom of skillet. Slowly add water and milk, stirring with wire whisk or fork. Bring slowly to boil and stir until it thickens. Salt and pepper, to taste. Place patties in gravy, turn heat down and simmer, covered for 25 minutes. Serve with mashed potatoes.

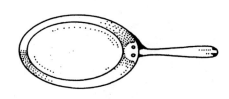

Chunked Venison

Bacon
Venison
2 C. water

Salt
Black pepper
½ C. Worcestershire sauce

Cut pieces of venison into 1-inch squares. Take a thin slice of bacon and cut it just long enough to wrap around the meat. Secure with a toothpick. Make about 2 dozen. Put in a cast-iron skillet. Add 2 C. water, salt, lots of black pepper, and ½ C. Worcestershire sauce. Boil rapidly until water is nearly gone. Reduce heat and cover skillet; continue cooking at lower temperature until meat is brown. The meat will be very rich.

Short Ribbed Venison

3 lb. venison short ribs
1 T. salt
1 qt. water
1 tsp. paprika
1 large onion (chopped)

½ C. catsup
¼ C. vinegar
2 T. water
2 tsp. chili powder
3 T. bacon drippings

Soak venison ribs in salt water solution for several hours or overnight. Wash the ribs after soaking and parboil for about 30 minutes in pressure cooker at 10 pounds pressure. Remove from pressure cooker and place in frying pan. Mix the last 7 ingredients together, pour over ribs, and bake at 375° for about 1 hour or until meat is tender and browned. Serves 4 to 6.

Venison Tipsy

2 lbs. venison steak
  (cut in ½-inch strips)
2 large onions
1 can sliced mushrooms
1 can golden mushroom soup

1 cube beef bouillon
½ C. water
1 oz. dry sherry
1 tsp. Worcestershire sauce
¼ lb. butter or oleo

Saute' sliced onions and mushrooms in melted butter in large skillet. Remove and set aside. Lightly brown venison in same pan. Dilute bouillon cube in water. When venison is brown add other ingredients starting with soup. Salt and pepper, to taste. Cover and simmer for 40 minutes. For a real treat serve over wild rice. If using venison chops, slice ¼-inch thick and use whole. Serves 4.

Tied in Knots Steak of Venison

1½-2 lbs. venison round steak
1 large white onion (diced)
1 lb. smoked bacon
Garlic salt

Oregano
2 (4 oz. ea.) cans mushrooms
Quick-mixing flour

Cut the venison steak into pieces approximately 4-inches by 3-inches. Hammer the pieces with a meat tenderizing tool until the size is approximately 6x4-inches. Layer the diced onion and 2 strips of uncooked bacon in the middle of each piece of meat. Sprinkle garlic salt and oregano sparginly on top of the bacon. Roll each piece into a bundle and secure with twine. Brown each bundle in a frying pan and then place in a Dutch oven. Add ¾ C. of water to the frying pan and scrape the pan. Then pour the contents over the meat in the Dutch oven. Simmer, covered, for about 3 hours, adding water if necessary. Remove the meat to heated platter and add mushrooms and quick-mixing flour to the Dutch oven to thicken the juices. Ladle the gravy over the meat and serve with wild rice. Serves 4.

Ribs BBQ

Your favorite barbecue sauce   *Venison ribs*

Prepare ribs as you would for baking, then remove ribs by cutting on inside of rib bone and peeling meat around ribs. Cut meat in strips; marinate rib meat in barbecue sauce overnight. Put meat in pint jars and can. (NOTE: Do not add salt to meat as there is enough in the sauce.) Process pints 75 minutes; quarts 90 minutes at 10 lbs. pressure.

Venison Steak ala Chicken

1 C. flour   *Venison round steak*
1 tsp. salt   *Oil*
¼ tsp. pepper

Tenderize steak in portion size pieces. Roll or shake steak in mixture of flour, salt, and pepper. Put oil in skillet 1/8-inch deep. Heat skillet over moderate temperature. Place steak in skillet to brown both sides. Remove steak and place in baking dish. Bake at 350° for 25 to 30 minutes. Serve.

Venison Cubes

When you are butchering your deer or when you have it butchered, save the end of the loin and cut it up in about 2-inch cubes.

1 lb. 2-inch cubed deer loin
2 medium green peppers (quartered)
16 morel mushrooms (whole) or
16 large button mushrooms

1 large onion (cut in 1/8's)
Italian salad dressing
Salt and pepper

Kabob all ingredients and cook over medium heat on grill turning twice, cook for 25 minutes, covering with Italian dressing each time you turn. Serves 4. Serve with burgundy wine.

Venison 'N 'Rooms

2-4 frozen venison steaks
4 qts. washed morel mushrooms
(less may be used)

2 T. butter
Salt & pepper, to taste
Oil for frying

Thaw venison steaks. If from an old deer, steaks should be marinated in a tenderizer and pounded until tender. Brown steaks on each side, in a large iron pan or on a griddle. Add thoroughly washed morels. The mushrooms may have to be washed four times to remove sand and other matter. Lower heat and simmer with salt, pepper, and butter until steaks are tender.

Super Sauteed Venison

1 lb. venison (well-trimmed)   Cooking oil
1 C. flour   Salt & pepper, to taste
1 T. dried minced onion

Cut venison into pieces about 3/8-inch thick and 1½-inch square. Dredge pieces in flour seasoned with salt and pepper. In heavy skillet, add 1/8-inch good cooking oil and heat on medium-high. Add onion evenly to hot oil and as soon as it begins to brown add the pieces of venison. Cook about 3 minutes or until juices appear on top side of meat. Turn and cook approximately 3 minutes and serve immediately. As this uses thin pieces of meat, be very careful to not overcook.

Pepper Steak on the Hoof

1 lb. deer round steak   1 C. green onion (sliced)
½ C. soy sauce   1 C. red or green peppers
1 clove garlic   (cut in 1-inch squares)
1½ tsp. grated fresh ginger or   2 stalks celery (sliced)
     ½ tsp. ground ginger   1 T. cornstarch
¼ C. salad oil   1 C. water
2 tomatoes (cut into wedges)

Cut round steak while still frozen into thin strips. Combine soy sauce, garlic, and ginger; add deer. Toss and set aside while preparing vegetables. Heat oil in large frying pan or wok. Add deer and toss over high heat until browned. Add vegetables. Toss until vegetables are tender-crisp, about 10 minutes. Mix cornstarch with water. Add to pan, stir, and cook until thickened. Add tomatoes and heat; serve with rice.

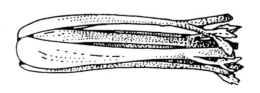

Kabobed Deer

1-2 lbs. venison steak (cubed)
Bottled French dressing
Mushrooms
Pineapple chunks

Greenpeppers (sliced)
Water chestnuts
Small onions

Place cubed venison in a bowl. Pour enough French dressing over meat to coat well. Marinate for 1 hour or more. Skewer meat, mushrooms, pineapple, peppers, water chestnuts, and onions on skewers according to individual taste. Grill over charcoal, basting lightly with dressing.

Venison Hotdish

1 lb. ground venison (browned)
1 C. diced celery
1 medium onion (chopped)
1 can cream of chicken soup
1 can cream of mushroom soup

2 C. warm water
½ C. uncooked rice
¼ C. soy sauce
Salt, to taste
Pepper, to taste

Mix all ingredients and pour into baking dish with a cover. Bake, covered for 30 minutes. Sprinkle a can of Chinese noodles over top and bake for 15 minutes longer.

Chapter VIII

BARBED WIRE FENCES

Speaking of concertina wire, I was going to do something about barbed wire.

I was going to devote a chapter to the issue of how best to climb those ever-present barbed wire fences.

The whole idea, however, is just too awful to contemplate at all. So, I'm not going to get into that at all. If you want to find out any information, or get any advice on how to cross a barbed wire fence while you're in the nude, you're gonna have to get that out of some other book. Maybe there's some sort of government pamphlet about that. That@$%#!&%*! government's got it all in it's head to tell ya anything else it's of a mind to.

And, besides crossin' barbed wire fences, there's another thing we ain't gonna talk about in this book.

An' that's snakebites.

I mean, even the thought of such a thing is bad enough when you're fully dressed. Just forget it, I ain't agonna talk about it.

Broiled Venison

2 lbs. venison steak   Salt and pepper, to taste
  (1-inch thick, which has   1 clove garlic
  been marinated)

Rub steak with garlic. Place on broiler pan and broil for 12 minutes. Then turn and brush with butter. Broil for 12 more minutes. Salt and pepper; serve hot. Note: Always serve venison very hot.

MARINADE FOR STEAK: ⅓ C. lemon juice, ⅔ C. oil, 2 cloves garlic (minced fine). Marinate steak for 8 to 10 hours in covered dish in refrigerator. Drain well before broiling. Serves 4 to 5.

NOTE: This marinade may be used to marinate venison roast or chops.

Roast on the Run

4 lbs. venison roast
3 strips bacon for larding
¼ lb. butter
½ C. water

1 tsp. lemon juice
1 C. sour cream
2 T. flour

Remove the skin and fat. Dredge in flour and sprinkle with salt and pepper. Brown venison in part of butter; put rest of butter in bottom of roaster. Lay bacon over venison meat. Roast in 350° oven until venison is tender, basting with butter and sour cream, a spoonful at a time. The roast should be pink inside and juicy. Remove roast to a hot platter. Brown flour in drippings; add water and cook for 10 minutes more. Add lemon juice, then strain. Serves 6 to 10.

NOTE: Venison may be rubbed with garlic before cooking if garlic flavor is desired. Whole onions may be placed around roast the last 20 minutes of roasting for variety.

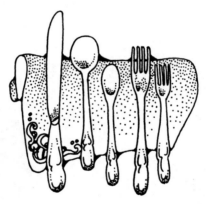

Venison 'N Beef

¼ beef meat

¾ venison meat

For every pound of meat, use 1 level teaspoon of Morton sausage seasoning. Mix thoroughly and grind into same container meat and seasonings were mixed. Sausage may be made into rolls and refrigerated. Slice into patties or may be stuffed into casings.

South of the Border Venison

1½ lbs. ground venison
2 cans kidney beans with liquid
1 qt. whole tomatoes
Garlic, if desired

1 medium onion (chopped)
1 tsp. chili powder
½ tsp. paprika

Cook in covered pan and simmer for 2 to 3 hours.

Leg of Venison

1 (3½ to 4 lb.) leg of venison
¼ lb. butter
Bacon strips
1 C. sour cream

2 T. flour
2 oz. bacon strips
½ C. water

Wipe meat carefully, draw off dry skin. Lay bacon strips on lean side of leg. Salt and pepper; dredge with flour. Melt butter and add meat and cook until light brown. Place meat on a few bacon strips in pan. Roast in moderate oven for 1 hour, basting often with cream. When meat is tender, remove from pan, and add flour to drippings. Cook for 2 minutes and add water. Cook for 5 minutes; strain and serve. Serves 6.

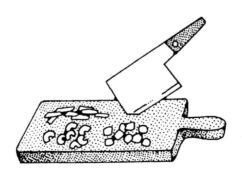

Deer Dip

1 lb. ground deerburger
2 lbs. Velveeta cheese
8 oz. jar hot picante sauce

1 can Golden Mushroom soup
3 cans sliced mushrooms
2-3 (4 oz. ea.) cans chopped
green chilies

Fry meat and drain any excess grease. Add all above ingredients and melt over low heat, stirring occasionally. Serve with nacho chips or corn chips.

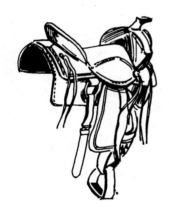

Saddle of Venison

Wipe a 4 pound saddle of venison with damp cloth. Tie in a roll. Rub ½ tsp. pepper and 1 tsp. salt into meat. Lay in pan, add 1 T. hot fat; add 1 T. water. Roast at 400° for 1 hour. Turn, baste frequently with broth. Serve with wild rice.

Jellystone Venison

6-8 venison loin chops
  (1-inch to 1½-inch thick)
4 T. butter
Salt and pepper
1 small onion (finely minced)
2 T. butter

½ C. consomme or stock
¼ C. tawny port
1½-2½ T. plump or red
  currant jelly
2 C. sour cream
  (room temp.)

Preheat broiler. Spread chops with softened butter and broil for 4 to 6 minutes on a side. Salt and pepper, to taste. Saute' the minced onion in the 2 T. butter for a couple of minutes, then add wine and stock. Cover over high heat to reduce by half. Stir jelly into sour cream until blended and then stir the mixture into onions and reduced liquid; do not boil. This dish best when one person makes the sauce and another puts the chops under the broiler just 4 to 5 minutes before the sour cream and jelly are stirred into the sauce. Chops are great if grilled on outdoor grill. Be careful not to overcook meat, it becomes tough.

Deer Steak on the Grill

6 deer loin steaks
  (cut 2-inches thick)

¼ lb. beef suet
Toothpicks

Cut meat on its side ½ to ¾ the way through horizontally. Insert beef suet. Pin meat shut with toothpicks. Grill on outdoor grill.

Venison Chops

6 venison chips (¾-inch thick)
1 onion (finely chopped)
Tarragon vinegar
Dash of Tabasco sauce

1 tsp. hot mustard
Dash of Worcestershire sauce
Chili sauce
½ C. bourbon whiskey

Cover chops with onion. Add vinegar to cover chops by ¼-inch in an iron skillet. Simmer until chops are tender. Combine remaining ingredients except whiskey and cook at low heat, stirring occasionally until thick. Add more vinegar or chili sauce, if needed. When the sauce is thick enough, spread generously on both sides of chops. Place in shallow pan and pour bourbon over them. Bake, uncovered at 350° for 1½ hours. Baste occasionally. Serves 3.

Venison Chili in a Hurry

1 qt. canned venison
1 qt. canned tomatoes
1 large can chili style beans

2 T. chili powder
Pepper
1 diced onion

Mix ingredients together; heat and serve. Great for hunting trips around campfire.

Jerked Venison

1 T. salt
¼ tsp. pepper
3 drops of Tabasco sauce
½ T. garlic salt

¼ T. Worcestershire sauce
Dash of oregano or thyme
1 lb. raw venison
Water

Cut venison into ¼-inch strips. Combine remaining ingredients and pour over meat, adding water, if needed to cover meat. Refrigerate overnight in mixture. Drain meat and pat dry. Bake at 120°-150° for 4 hours.

Yuppie Venison

1 small container plain yogurt
1 large onion (diced)

2 T. Lawry's seasoned salt
2-3 lbs. venison steaks or chops

Combine all but meat in bowl. Pour into strong plastic bag. Add venison and seal bag. Squeeze to distribute marinade over meat. Refrigerate for 3 to 4 hours or overnight, turning bag occasionally. Grill or broil meat to your taste.

Venison and Rice

1½ lbs. venison
1½ T. vegetable oil
2 large onions (cut in rings)
4 ozs. sliced mushrooms

1 can cream of mushroom soup
½ C. dry sherry
1½ tsp. garlic salt
3 C. hot cooked rice

Cut venison in thin strips. Brown meat in oil. Add onions and saute' until tender-crisp. Blend all but rice. Pour over venison. Reduce heat and simmer for 1 hour or until tender or cover and bake at 350° until tender. Serve over rice.

More Jerked Venison

1 T. salt
¼ tsp. pepper
3 drops of Tabasco sauce
½ T. garlic salt

¼ T. Worcestershire sauce
Dash of oregano or thyme
1 lb. raw venison
Water

Cut venison into ¼-inch strips. Combine remaining ingredients and pour over meat, adding water, if needed to cover meat. Refrigerate overnight in mixture. Drain meat and pat dry. Bake at 120°-150° for 4 hours.

Chapter IX

SNOBBERY SNIPPIN'

Unfortunately, even the noble sport of hunting is afflicted with the disease of snobbery.

This snobbery affliction can rear its ugly head about dress, equipment or one's experiences.

One of the most important of the advantages of romping around the fields and streams au naturel is that it prevents one from falling into the trap of clothes snobbery. It is, after all, difficult to leave your companions with the impression that your hunting jacket was custom made by some overpriced European tailor when you don't have one on. Your skin doesn't sport any little brand name tags that would impress anyone.

On the other hand, hunting in the nude enables you to engage in a fetching little exercise in reverse snobbery. You can do this by noticing the folks that do practice clothes snobbery ... "are still wearing clothes ... just like **everybody** else.".

Such tactics have been known to cause clothes to fly faster than they do in an hourly rate No-Tell Motel in

East St. Louis. Lots of folks just can't get shed of 'em fast enough there.

It is useful to keep in mind that it is impossible to embarrass a clothes snob nearly as much as he/she deserves.

Venison Meatballs

1 lb. ground venison
¼ tsp. oregano
½ tsp. garlic salt
1 jar favorite barbecue sauce

Salt, pepper, and onion salt
   (to taste)
3 small squares crackers
   (in fine crumbs)

Mix all ingredients and form into meatballs. Bake for 15 to 20 minutes; remove from oven. Drain grease and cover with barbecue sauce. Keep warm while serving.

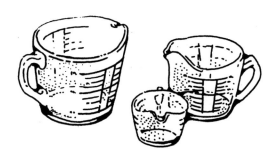

Venison Chili Dip

2 lbs. ground venison
2 lbs. Velveeta cheese
½ C. sliced jalapeno (or to taste)

2 cans Hormel Chili
   without beans

Brown venison and drain. Cube Velveeta cheese. Place all ingredients in crock pot on high heat, stirring occasionally. Turn to low heat when cheese is melted. Serve warm with tortilla chips.

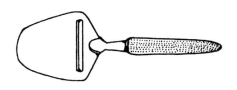

Deer in a Can

Deer meat
Beef bouillon cubes

Salt
Beef suet

Cut meat small enough to fit in quart or pint jars. Fill jars 4/5 full of deer meat. For quarts, add 2 beef bouillon cubes and 1 tsp. salt; add beef suet to remaining space in jar leaving ½-inch air space. Place rings and flats on jars and put in pressure canner at 10 lbs. for 90 minutes (quarts); 70 minuts (pints). Great for stews and sandwiches!

Tomato Eggplant Vension Casserole

1 qt. canned deer
2 T. oil
½ tsp. oregano
1 T. flour

1 medium eggplant
1 C. sharp cheese (grated)
½ C. chopped onion
2 large tomatoes (sliced)

Peel and cube eggplant. Boil in salt water until tender, not soft. Drain and set aside. Put canned deer in casserole dish and cover with tomato slices. Add eggplant and season with oregano and top with cheese. Bake at 350° for 30 to 40 minutes.

Stewed Bambi

1 jar canned deer
2 medium-size cans mixed
  vegetables
2 medium potatoes (cut-up small)

2 stalks celery (cut-up)
½ C. water
3 bay leaves

Combine ingredients in crock pot. Cook on Low for 6 to 8 hours or High for 3 to 6 hours. Remove bay leaves before eating. If any leftovers, put in container and freeze for a meal another day.

Barbecue Venison Sandwiches

1 jar canned deer

Barbecue sauce

Remove beef suet from canned deer. Add barbecue sauce and warm through. Serve on buns.

Amigo Venison

1 pt. canned venison
¼ C. chopped onion
4 eggs
1 (8 oz.) can tomato sauce
1 (5⅓ oz.) can evaporated milk

1 (1½ oz.) env. enchilada
   sauce mix
⅓ C. sliced pitted ripe olives
2 C. tortilla corn chips
1 C. shredded Cheddar cheese

In skillet cook meat and onion until onions are tender. Drain and spread meat mixture in a 10x6x2-inch baking dish. Beat together eggs, tomato sauce, evaporated milk, and enchilada sauce mix; pour over meat. Sprinkle with olive slices and top with chips. Bake, uncovered at 350° until center is set, 20 to 25 minutes. Sprinkle with cheese and bake until cheese melts, 3 to 5 minutes. Makes 6 servings. (Can substitute ground venison for canned and cook until brown with onions.)

Even More Jerked Venison

1½ lbs. flank steak
1 tsp. seasoned salt
1 T. liquid smoke
1 tsp. Tender Quick salt
¼ C. soy sauce

⅓ tsp. garlic salt or powder
⅓ tsp. black pepper
1 tsp. Accent
1 tsp. onion powder or salt
¼ C. Worcestershire sauce

Trim off all fat from meat. Cut meat into 1/8-inch to ¼-inch thick pieces (cuts better if partially frozen). Combine seasoning and sauces. Put meat in a 9x9x2-inch glass pan and cover with seasoning and sauce mixture. Let set overnight. Dry in oven at 140° for 6 to 8 hours. (NOTE: Meat should be in a single layer.) Makes about ½ lb.

Dear Heart

PICKLING SOLUTION:
3 C. white vinegar
1 C. water

3 tsp. (heaping) pickling spice
¾ C. white sugar

Simmer for 30 minutes. Remove fat from heart and boil for 2 hours. Put in pickling solution and refrigerate. Can be eaten in 24 hours.

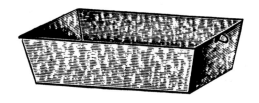

Hot Flash Venison

3 lbs. ground venison
1 medium onion
3 medium cans kidney beans
1 jar Pace picante sauce (hot)

½ can tomato soup
Salt and pepper, to taste
1 C. jalapeno peppers (sliced)

Brown meat, onion, salt, pepper, and hot peppers. Add remaining ingredients and simmer for ½ hour.

Mexican Venison

1 lb. ground venison
4 C. diced potatoes
1 can chili beans
1 can stewed tomatoes

Tomato juice
Chili powder
Onion, to taste

Boil potatoes until almost done. Brown ground venison and onions, if desired. Pour chili beans and tomatoes into large pan; add browned venison and boiled potatoes. Season, to taste and then add tomato juice to desired consistency Simmer for at least ½ hour.

Oven Stew Venison

2 C. potatoes (diced)
2 C. carrots (sliced)
2 C. celery (diced)
1 large onion (diced)
Salt and pepper, to taste

1½ lbs. venison
  (cut into bite-size pieces)
1 large or 2 small cans
  tomato soup

Mix all ingredients together in large baking dish with a lid. Bake, covered at 275° for 5 hours. Do not uncover or stir.

Stroganoff, Venison . . . In a Hurry

1 qt. canned venison
½ C. chopped onion
3 C. dry noodles
3 T. tomato juice

1 T. pepper
2 tsp. Worcestershire sauce
1 (8 oz.) carton sour cream

In Dutch oven, shred canned venison. Add onion and dry noodles. Mix and add tomato juice, pepper, and Worcestershire sauce. Swing over low coals, cover, and simmer for 30 minutes; add sour cream. Reheat a few minutes and serve. You can cook on top of stove but cooking over a wood fire adds extra flavor to this easy dish.

99

More Sandwiches with Venison

2 lbs. venison round steak
½ lb. bacon
1 C. chopped onion
2 cloves garlic (minced)
1 C. ketchup

½ C. red wine vinegar
¼ C. Worcestershire sauce
¼ C. brown sugar
Salt & pepper
12 buns

Slice venison round steak in 1/8-inch strips 4-inches long. In bottom of Dutch oven cook bacon until crisp. Remove, crumble, and set aside. In a bowl mix all ingredients, except venison. Salt and pepper, to taste. Brown venison in bacon drippings and pour off grease. Add bowlful of ingredients to venison; stir well. Cover tightly and simmer for 1 hour or until tender, stirring occasionally. Serve in buns with extra sauce. Can cook in fire over low coals or on Coleman Stove. Serves 6.

Suet Pudding

1½ C. kidney suet (beef)
5 C. flour
Salt & pepper
2 lbs. sirloin or round steak
  (venison is good, too)

1 good sliced onion
1 old dish towel or diaper
1 string

Mix flour and suet. Add 1 tsp. salt and 1 tsp. pepper and add water to make dough. Cut-up meat in 1-inch squares and chop onion. Spread dough about 1-inch thick on towel or diaper and place meat and onion in middle. Pull dough up around meat until completely covered and tie with string making several rounds to secure. Place in boiling pot with plate upside down in bottom and cover with water with 1 tsp. salt added. Boil for 4 hours, turning once. Remove from cloth by cutting string. Slice and serve covered with juice. Serve with bread and butter and burgundy wine. Serves 6.

Chapter X

FIELD DRESSED

I t's our language that really strikes me as being the source of an awfully lot of confusion and an awfully lot of our problems.

I mean, think about it. Some of the mental gymnastics that our language demands of us is downright exhausting.

At first blush it all seems pretty much straight forward. Certain words are supposed to represent certain things. When you see the word *dog*, you immediately think of those four legged critters with tongues approximately a jillion times as big as their brains.

Likewise, the word *chair* elicits thoughts of another four-legged creature, but one distinctly different than a dog. Both of these words essentially excludes all meanings other than the obvious ones.

But, then, on the other hand, things can get downright confusing.

Take, for example, a nude hunter who has bagged a deer, meaning, of course... shot a deer, and has field dressed the critter.

There the two of them are, the hunter, and the critter, both of them in their birthday suits, both of 'em unencumbered with any clothes, be it pants or a dress. Yet the critter is called field dressed, when, in fact, bein' field

dressed has nothing to do at all with a dress. No dress, no shirt, no trousers, no nothing has been put on it. In fact, stuff has been taken away.

I don't understand it at all; one of 'em *dressed*, and the other isn't, yet they are both stark naked.

Somebody's gotta take the blame for this mess.

Ribby Deer in the Oven

4 lbs. venison ribs
1 T. butter
1 clove garlic
½ C. catsup
⅓ C. chili sauce
2 T. brown sugar
2 T. chopped onions

1 T. Worcestershire sauce
1 T. prepared mustard
1 tsp. celery salt
¼ tsp. salt
Dash of hot pepper sauce
2 T. Real Lemon juice

Simmer cut-up in enough salt water to cover until nearly tender, about 1 hour. In saucepan, melt butter. Add clove of garlic (crushed) and cook 4 to 5 minutes. Add the rest of the ingredients and bring to a boil. Drain ribs, place in shallow pan, pour boiling sauce over ribs. Bake at 350° for 20 minutes or until tender, basting often with sauce. Serves 6 to 8.

Squashy Venison

1 medium acorn squash
1 pt. canned venison or
  ½ lb. ground venison
2 T. chopped onion
2 T. chopped celery
2 T. all-purpose flour

¼ tsp. salt
¼ tsp. ground sage
¾ C. milk
½ C. cooked rice
¼ C. shredded sharp cheese
Pepper

Cut squash in half and discard seeds. Sprinkle squash with a little salt. Bake, cut side down in small baking dish at 350° until tender, 45 to 50 minutes. Cook meat, onion, and celery until onions are clear; drain. Stir in flour, salt, and sage. Add milk. Cook and stir until thickened and bubbly. Stir in rice. Turn squash side up in dish; fill and bake, uncovered at 350° for 30 minutes. Sprinkle with pepper and top with cheese. Bake until cheese melts, about 3 minutes. Serves 2.

Venison Stew

2 lbs. lean venison (1-inch cubes)
3 T. cooking oil
1 medium onion (cut small)
3 stalks celery (cut ¾-inch pieces)
2 cloves garlic (diced)
4 T. flour
1 (16 oz.) can tomatoes (chopped)
6-10 drops Tabasco sauce

1 (10 oz.) can tomato juice or V-8
1 (12 oz.) can beer
½ tsp. thyme
2 tsp. Worcestershire sauce
3 carrots (cut in ½-inch chunks)
2 C. potatoes (cut ½-inch)
1 C. beef stock or bouillon
    stock brought to a boil

Brown venison in oil in heavy pot. Remove meat and add onions, celery, and garlic to remaining oil and juices; cook until tender. Do not brown. Add flour and stir in well. Add boiling stock, stirring until smooth. Add tomatoes, juices, beer, spices, and venison; stir until mixed. Reduce heat and simmer for 1 hour. Add carrots and simmer for 1 hour more, covered. Add potatoes and cook until tender, about 45 minutes. Serves 6 to 8.

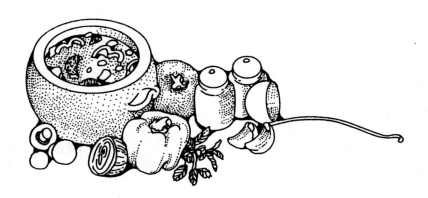

Saucy Venison

Warm a glass of currant jelly in half as much port wine and serve hot with venison.

CURRANT JELLY SAUCE:

2 T. butter or bacon fat   ¼ tsp. salt
3 T. flour   1/8 tsp. black pepper
½ glass currant jelly (4 oz.)   2 T. sherry wine
1 C. water or beef stock

Mix seasoning with flour and brown butter and flour together. Add stock of water gradually, bringing to boiling point for a few minutes. Melt currant jelly in sauce and season with 2 T. sherry wine.

Venison Round Steak Casserole with Dumplings

1 venison round steak (cubed)   ¼ tsp. pepper
¼ C. flour   Onion, to taste
1 tsp. salt   2 cans cream of chicken soup
¼ tsp. paprika   1 soup can of water

Coat meat with flour and seasonings. Brown meat and add onions and soup can of water. Bake at 350° for 40 to 45 minutes.

DUMPLINGS:

2 C. flour   ½ tsp. salt
4 tsp. baking powder

Stir into these 3 ingredients ¾ C. milk and ¼ C. oil. Add 1 tsp. poultry seasoning and 1 T. celery seed. Drop mixture on roast to form dumplings. Bake for 15 to 20 minutes longer.

Assorted Stuff I Can't Figure Where to Put Anywhere Else

Stewed Stew

2 lbs. chuck of any big game meat
  (cut in pieces)
3 T. salad oil
2 cloves garlic (minced)
3 large onions (quartered)
1 (6 oz.) can tomato paste
1 T. flour
1 tsp. chili powder
1 tsp. oregano

1 tsp. rosemary
1½ T. seasoned salt
2 (16 oz. ea.) cans stewed
  tomatoes
½ C. snipped celery or parsley
1 C. water
3 medium carrots
½ lb. macaroni
½ C. shredded Parmesan cheese

In large Dutch oven heat salad oil and brown meat on all sides. Add garlic onion and saute' well, turning frequently. Stir in tomato paste, flour, chili powder, oregano, rosemary, seasoned salt, tomatoes, and celery or parsley. Add water and simmer covered for 1 hour and 15 minutes. Skim off fat, if necessary. Add carrots and simmer for 45 minutes longer. Meanwhile, cook macaroni, as package directs. Drain it well and stir into stew with Parmesan cheese. Serves 6.

Big Critter Heart

Heart of deer, elk, etc.
Salt & pepper

Bay leaf if available

Put heart in pot large enough to cover heart with water. Salt and pepper, to taste and add bay leaf. Bring to a boil and then simmer for about 1 hour. Let cool after done. Slice in thin pieces and use as lunch meat or serve for snacks.

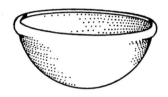

Fried Liver

Soak liver in salt water to help remove all blood. Slice liver into pieces about 3/8-inch thick and return to clean salt water. While slicing clean liver of all fat and tough veins, etc. In large skillet heat grease and slice two or three large onions cooking until onions are about half done. At this time drain liver and roll in flour seasoned with salt and pepper. As soon as liver is coated add to the hot grease. Push all of the onions to one side stirring occasionally. Cook liver quickly but not too long. Liver has its best taste when still slightly pink or just past that stage. (In my opinion most liver is ruined because it is cooked too long.)

BBQ Loin

3½-4 lbs. loin   Marinade
   (bear, antelope, deer, elk)

Inject roast with marinade. Heat coals to hot or gas grill on high. Salt and pepper loin and sear over coals. Reduce heat and close lid on grill. Cook for 1½ hours unless bear, then cook for 2½ hours. Serve on warmed serving platter with additional marinade added. Serve with baked potato and applesauce. Serves 6.

Stuffed Stuff

½ loaf dried bread   Salt and pepper
1 medium onion (chopped)   6 (1-inch ea.) chops from
½ tsp. sage   elk, deer, moose
2 tsp. butter

Break bread into bowl. Add chopped onion, ½ tsp. sage, 2 tsp. melted butter, salt, and pepper. Mix while adding water to make sticky (not soggy). Butterfly chops or 1-inch slices of loin. Stuff chops and hold dressing in with toothpick. Sprinkle with flour and brown. Reduce heat to 350°. Add ½ C. of water; cover and cook for 1½ hours. Serve with au gratin potatoes and your favorite salad. Serves 6.

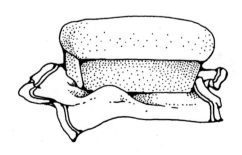

Chapter XI

TICKLED PINK

Harold Buffington's experience when he was out deer hunting in Page County in '93 certainly dramatizes our need to get hospital costs under control.

Since Harold was in the buff, he was faced with the problem that comes to those who choose to do their deer hunting au naturel. Yes, it was that old no-pockets problem.

This lack of pockets led Harold to temporarily stash his deer tags around his wrist, just barely securing it with the adhesive on the back of it. He put it there on his wrist where he'd know where it was and could use it if he lucked out and got a deer that day.

Harold had gotten a stern lecture from his doctor about someone or the other of his bad habits and had gotten stuck in the hospital for some lab tests.

He had just gotten out of the hospital that morning. He had been properly tagged with one of those little plastic bracelets with his name and social security number on it.

In the hustle and bustle of getting ready to go deer hunting, Harold hadn't removed the tag, so he had his wrists festooned with two tags, each of them not dramatically different in appearance from the other. One was a souvenir of his hospital stay and one was destined for the deer he hoped to get that evening.

Harold lucked out and bagged a real nice buck, his fifth deer in as many years of hunting.

And, you deer hunters out there know how it is when you get your deer. Things get pretty exciting 'long about then.

You have to find the critter after you get him, make sure he's down for the count, and so forth. There's always the concern lest the deer will enjoy a revival of some sort and turn the table on you, doing all kinds of nasty things with those sharp antlers. That concern is even more of a factor when you're standing there in your birthday suit, of course.

It was that few minutes of excitement that led to Harold making the little mistake that he did. In the excitement of the moment he took the wrong tag off of his wrist, slapped it on the ankle of his buck, and pitched the other tag in the ditch. Things had to get done, and he sure didn't have time to be just real careful about that useless old tag he had forgotten to discard earlier.

So Harold loaded his prize up on the top of his car and bombed off to the inspection station where he was obligated to check in with the buck.

The gal there in charge of recording the tag information for the state records was a bit taken aback by the sight of a fellow bringing in a deer, both him and the deer bein' buck naked.

Maybe if she hadn't been so distracted by that situation she would have been a little more careful in her noticing the tag she was processing. Some folks are easily distracted if their mind's not on their work, don't ya know?

Well, anyway, the information from that "deer tag" on the leg of that animal found its way into the computer system of the State of Illinois and the deer found his way into Harold's freezer.

One would have thought that would be the end of it, but it wasn't. While decent folks were sleeping, those magic computers were busy working through the night, screwing things up as best they could.

And, they did a real good job on Harold's hospital tag. Somehow the information got shuffled over into the medical records portion of the state bureaucracy. From there that innocent appearing information of Harold's name and social security number got mixed up with the hospital records from a Chicago hospital.

Well, once that happened the die was cast. Within a short time Harold reaped the rewards of his inattentiveness that day out in the woods when he put the wrong tag on that buck.

113

The first one of the bills he got was one of those "We're-just-tickled-pink-to-serve-your-needs" type of things.

The next one was a motherly reminder that nice boys pay their bills on time. The third one spoke of taking Harold's first born unless he came through with the cash.

The cash, of course, was for the bill he had run up there in that Chicago hospital. There was the small matter of those $23.00 aspirins, six of those doctor's visits that consisted of a cute little wave from the doorway as the man in green ambled by. All that was, of course, added to the x-rays made the total cost something that dwarfed the gross national product of a medium sized nation.

The fact that Harold hadn't been in a Chicago hospital ever, or even in Chicago itself since his high school senior trip back in '52, didn't faze the computer one little bit. That machine knew a deadbeat when it saw one.

We don't know how Harold's fight with the bureaucracy came out, but he did report that thereafter he was awfully *awfully* careful not to leave a hospital anymore with that little plastic tag still on his wrist.

Smothered Steak

6 venison loin steaks (butterflied)
1 large green pepper (sliced)
1 large onion (sliced)

8 oz. fresh mushrooms (sliced)
Salt and pepper, to taste
6 slices provolone cheese

Cook venison steaks the way you like them, either broiled or cooked in a little oil in a skillet, seasoned to taste. In a seperate skillet, saute' peppers, onions, and mushrooms in oil or butter. Do not cook all the way done. Put steaks on a broiled pan and cover each with sauteed' vegetables and top with the provolone cheese. Place under broiler until cheese melts and just turns golden brown.

Chili

4 T. butter or drippings
1 lb. game 'burger'
2 sliced onions
Chili powder, to taste

1 shredded green pepper
(if desired)
2 (15 oz. ea.) cans Mexican
beans in chili gravy

Brown meat and onions in fat (start with frozen meat, if necessary), breaking the meat in small pieces as it browns; drain. Add green pepper and chili beans. Cover and simmer for 10 minutes. Check seasoning and add more chili powder, if desired and simmer for 10 minutes more.

Canned Critter

1 animal

Cube pieces of meat. Pack raw meat tightly in jars. Put lids on. Pressure cook for 90 minutes at 10 lbs. for quarts; 75 minutes at 10 lbs. for pints. Great for round steaks, just drop them in wide mouth quart jars. To use pour out in skillet and reheat with your choice of mushrooms, mushroom soup, onions or your favorite Swiss steak recipe. Quick and easy! Cubed meat is great in chili, casserole dishes, over noodles or biscuits, in stews and soups, etc.

Jerky in a Hurry

Any amount of meat (up to 10 lbs.,   *½ pt. vinegar*
    cut into ¼-inch strips)   *2 C. salt*
2 qts. water   *2 T. black pepper*

Add all ingredients and boil for 5 minutes. Roll any excess moisture from meat with a rolling pin or by hand. Place on oven racks and cook for 1½ to 2 hours at 200° with door open (cracked) on oven. Remove meat and paint with basting brush using A-1 sauce or open pit sauce or horseradish and ketchup mixture or other seasoned sauces.

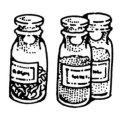

Poached Poach

8 English muffins
8 slices American cheese

16 slices Canadian bacon
8 eggs

Toast English muffins and fry Canadian bacon while poaching eggs. Place Canadian bacon on muffins. Cover with cheese and top with poached egg. Quick and easy in camp. Serves 4.

Up and At'em Breakfast

1 fresh liver (deer, elk, antelope)
1 onion (chopped)
6 eggs

1 green pepper (chopped)
Salt & pepper
Frying oil

Peel skin off fresh liver; soak in salt water overnight. Cut liver into small pieces. Put liver, chopped onion, and green pepper into frying pan (large) and fry until liver is well done. Add eggs and stir until eggs are cooked. Salt and pepper, to own taste.

Stove Top Baked Beans

1 (31 oz.) can pork & beans
6 ozs. American cheese (cubed)
¼ C. Minute Rice
1 T. mustard

¼ C. brown sugar (packed)
¼ C. catsup
1 tsp. dried minced onion

Combine all ingredients in 2-quart saucepan. Cook over medium-low heat for approximately 1 hour, stirring occasionally. If cooking over a campfire, watch that hot spots don't scorch the cheese. Serves 6.

Fish in Foil

8 fillets of walleye,
  smallmouth bass
4 C. cooked Minute Rice
Juice of 1 lemon
¼ lb. butter

Garlic salt
Seasoned salt
Pepper
2 medium onions

Mix melted butter with juice of 1 lemon. Cross 2 pieces of 18-inch foil per person. Place onion slices on foil and salt and pepper. Place fillet on onions and sprinkle with seasoned salt and garlic salt. Cover with rice and lemon juice. Put several pats of butter on rice. Cover with onion and second fillet, season fish and pour juice and butter over top. Seal foil and place in coals of fire for 40 minutes. Slit top and let fish get brown and serve. Serves 4.

Broiled Fish

3 lbs. pan-dressed small fish
2 tsp. salt
Dash of pepper

⅓ C. chopped onion
⅓ C. chopped parsley
3 strips bacon (cut in half)

Clean, wash, and dry fish. Prepare 6 pieces of heavy-duty aluminum foil, 12x12-inches each. Grease lightly. Divide fish into 6 portions. Place fish on foil. Sprinkle with salt and pepper. Place onion and parsley on fish. Top with bacon. Bring the foil up over the food and close all edges with tight folds. Make 6 packages. Place packages on a grill about 4-inches from hot coals. Cook for 10 to 15 minutes or until fish flakes easily when tested with a fork.

Fried Fowl

¼ C. margarine
¼ tsp. thyme
¼ C. chopped onion
1 tsp. dried parsley

1 C. apple juice
1 tsp. salt
1/8 tsp. paprika
Flour

Quarter bird and roll in flour. Melt the margarine in a heavy frypan. When it is hot brown the fowl. Sprinkle on the thyme. Cover and cook over low heat for 10 minutes. Mix the chopped onion, dried parsley, and cup of juice which may be from cooked dried apples. Cover and keep simmering for 1 hour. About 10 minutes before the cooking is finished, sprinkle on salt and paprika. A good accompaniment is rice.

Orange Sauce

1½ C. beef stock
2 oranges
1 lemon
¼ C. butter
½ C. water

¼ C. flour
½ tsp. salt
Dash cayenne pepper
2 T. sherry wine

Slice the peel of 1 orange as fine as possible. Cook in water for 5 minutes; put in saucepan with 1 C. beef stock. Brown the butter and add flour and seasonings. Stir until browned. Add rest of beef stock. Gradually add the juice of lemon and oranges, then orange rind mixture. Boil a few minutes. Just before serving add sherry. You may add a spoonful of currant jelly. Serve hot over roasted duck.

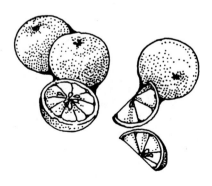

Hush Puppies

2 C. cornmeal
½ C. water
1½ C. milk

2 tsp. baking powder
1 tsp. salt
1 medium onion (diced)

Mix all ingredients and drop by teaspoonfuls into very hot deep fat. Fry until golden brown.

Beer Batter

1 C. flour
½ tsp. sugar
½ tsp. salt

1 egg
1 C. cold beer
2 T. oil

Beat ingredients. Dip fish in batter and fry in hot oil (375°) until golden brown. Drain on paper towels.

Grounded Liver

½ lb. livers (adjust other
    ingredients to match quantity
    of livers)
1 onion (diced)
Clove of garlic
2 hard-boiled eggs (finely diced)
1 T. grated onion

2 T. mayonnaise
1 tsp. vinegar
Dash of Worcestershire sauce
Salt and pepper, to taste
½ tsp. dry mustard
Pinch of sugar

Save all livers (duck, quail, pneasant, etc.). Simmer in salted water for ½
hour. Add onion and clove of garlic. Cook slowly for 1 hour. Remove liver
and discard garlic clove. Mash liver and mix with eggs, grated onion, mayonnaise, vinegar, Worcestershire sauce, salt, pepper, dry mustard, and sugar.
Serve on crackers.

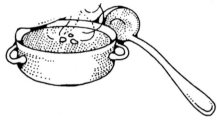

Bird in a Pot Stew

2 whole game birds
¼ C. butter or margarine
4 cubes chicken bouillon
4 C. water
1 small pkg. frozen broccoli or
    equivalent amount of fresh
    broccoli (chopped)
½ C. milk

4 medium carrots
    (peeled & sliced)
1 small onion
2 medium potatoes
    (unpeeled, scrubbed & cubed)
1 handful egg noodles
1 can mushroom soup

Place water, bouillon, butter, and meat in large pot. Simmer until meat is
tender (about 45 minutes), adding water if necessary. Remove the meat from
the broth; add the vegetables and egg noodles and simmer until all are tender.
While vegetables are cooking, remove meat from the bones; tear it into small
pieces and add to broth. Add soup and milk to broth and heat through. Make
sure the stew does not come to a boil. Serves 4.

Grilled Dove

Dove breast (split)
Jalapeno peppers (sliced)
1 stick butter or oleo (melted)

¼ C. lemon juice
Bacon

Fill dove breast with peppers. Wrap with 1 slice of bacon. Secure with toothpick through middle to hold together. Place on BBQ grill on low flame. Turn and baste often with butter and lemon juice mixed.

Roast Turkey

Roast turkey with favorite stuffing. For more flavor and juiciness, roast breast down; if roasted breast up, cover breast with strips of bacon or fat salt pork or melted butter. Roast in moderate oven, 20 to 25 minutes per pound.

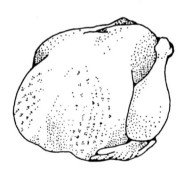

Partridge ala Lemon

3 partridges
½ C. wine

¼ C. lemon juice

Place clean, larded bird in greased casserole; add lemon juice and bake at 350° for 15 minutes. Add wine, cover, and cook until tender or about 25 minutes. Serve with lemon sauce. Serves 6.

Broiled Grouse

Parboil grouse for 30 minutes. Baste with melted margarine and place under broiler until tender.

Rice 'N Roast Pigeon Breasts

6 slices bacon
¾ C. celery (diced)
1 onion (chopped)
2 C. uncooked rice
4 C. chicken stock

4 eggs
Salt and pepper
4 pigeon breasts
Mustard pickle juice

Dice bacon and fry crisp. Remove bacon and add onion and celery to bacon drippings; brown lightly. Boil rice in chicken stock; add onions and celery. Beat eggs and add. Season to taste. In greased casserole, arrange pigeons. Pile mounds of rice mixture on breasts and around. Bake at 325° for 45 to 60 minutes. Baste every 15 minutes with mustard pickle juice.

Pigeon Pots

6 pigeons or doves
4 C. sage stuffing
3 slices bacon
1 carrot (diced)
1 onion (diced)
1 tsp. parsley (chopped)

4 C. hot water with 2 chicken
  bouillon cubes added
¼ C. oleo
¼ C. flour
6 slices buttered toast

Place birds in roaster, stuff with dressing and lay birds on bacon. Add carrots, onions, and parsley. Add water mixed with bouillon, 2 cups. Cover and bake for 2 to 3 hours. Melt fat and blend in flour and add remaining 2 C. stock. Cook this separately in saucepan. Serve each bird on toast with vegetables and pour gravy over.

Chapter XII

A NOTE OF CAUTION

You know how it is with squirrels. They've got teeth and claws that won't quit. Squirrels can hurt like all get out and do so on all five corners.

Nude hunters, by definition, cannot put their game in a coat pocket. Because of that, the nude hunter will be tempted to carry a squirrel by the tail down by his or her side.

"Down by one's side" is probably the last place in the world that one would want to dangle an animal that chews through telephone lines as a hobby and nibbles black walnuts into little bitty pieces just for the heck of it.

It is far better to sling the little fellow over a shoulder and carry him that way. A knawed-on shoulder wouldn't be pleasant, but would be a big step up from what could

happen. Folks have been known to recover quite nicely from the bites on the shoulder or back from a suddenly-got-well squirrel.

Spiced Pigeons with Hot Sauce

6 pigeons
Make 4 C. sage dressing
6 link sausages
⅔ C. salad olives
2 cloves garlic (minced)
1 can mushroom pieces

3 T. salad oil
½ tsp. basil
1 (8 oz.) can tomato sauce
½ tsp. chopped parsley
1 tsp. chopped onion
¼ tsp. hot sauce (if desired)

Stuff pigeons with dressing. Brown sausages, remove, and add remaining ingredients and simmer for 10 minutes. Place pigeons in roaster and arrange sausages around. Pour over the tomato sauce, cover, and roast at 400° for 30 minutes; basting every 20 minutes. Reduce heat to 375° and roast for 40 minutes more basting every 10 minutes. Serve with cooked rice.

Beaver Tail Roast

1 Beaver tail
1 C. red wine
1 C. water
1 large onion (chopped)
Cracker crumbs
Lemon juice

½ C. vinegar
1 tsp. salt
Flour
Egg
3 T. melted butter

Marinate tail for 24 hours in wine, water, and onion. Dry tail and scrape carefully. Parboil until tender in enough water to cover. To the water add ½ C. vinegar and 1 tsp. salt. Dry tail again. Dust with flour and dip into beaten eggs, then cracker crumbs. Pour 3 T. melted butter over tail. Roast on rack in a 350° oven until brown and tender. Serve with hot lemon juice. Serves 2.

Roast Beaver

A beaver has scent glands located between the forelegs, under the thighs, and along the spine. These should be carefully removed immediately after the animal has been skinned, but be sure not to cut into them. Remove all surface fat and cover meat with a solution of 1 tsp. soda to 1 qt. water. Simmer for 10 minutes. Put meat in roaster, cover with sliced onions, strips of bacon, salt, and roast in moderate oven (350°). Beaver should be cooked until meat falls off the bones.

Beaver Patties

1 beaver (ground)
1 onion (chopped)
½ tsp. celery salt
3 T. margarine

½ tsp. salt
Black pepper, to taste
¼ C. milk
¼ C. bread crumbs

Mix all ingredients together, except the margarine. Melt margarine in fry pan; form patties and fry in hot oil as you would a hamburger. Fry until well done. For added flavor, pour a can of your favorite soup over the beaver burgers and simmer for 20 minutes.

Clam Chowder

3 C. chicken broth
⅓ C. diced celery
1 carrot (diced)
1 dozen fresh clams or
   1 (10½ oz.) can clams
3 T. butter

2 C. diced raw, peeled potatoes
2 T. chopped onion
2 T. flour
½ C. Half & Half
Salt and pepper, to taste

Steam fresh clams and pry open. Drain off and measure liquid so you have 1 cup. Put carrots, potatoes, and celery into chicken broth. Cover and cook slowly until tender. Then saute' clams and onions in butter for 5 minutes to just light brown. Blend flour evenly into the mixture. Add broth and vegetables gradually, stirring to keep smooth. Add clam broth, cream, and seasonings. Reheat just to boiling and serve. Makes 8 cups.

Corned Clam Casserole

3 eggs (beaten)
1 T. minced onion
1 C. cream-style corn
1 (7 oz.) can clam
½ tsp. chopped parsley
½ C. croutons

1 T. butter
1½ T. diced pimientos
Dash of cayenne pepper
Salt and pepper, to taste
Milk

Drain liquid from clam and add enough milk to make 1 cup. Combine with beaten eggs. Add all remaining ingredients and pour into greased casserole. Bake at 375° until set firm, about 45 minutes. Serves 6.

Scalloped Clams

1½ C. minced clams or
   canned clams
2 T. minced onions
½ C. butter
½ C. bread crumbs or
   cracker crumbs

Salt and white pepper, to taste
2 T. chopped parsley
⅓ C. milk
¼ tsp. lemon
¼ tsp. paprika

Melt butter; add crumbs, salt, pepper, parsley, and paprika. Mix, reserving ⅓ for topping. Mix remainder with clams, milk, lemon juice, and onions. Pour in oiled casserole. Sprinkle with crumbs and dot with butter. Bake at 375°, uncovered for 25 minutes.

Clams 'N Toast

1 C. minced clams
1 C. milk
2 T. flour
2 T. butter

1 tsp. chives
1 C. Half & Half milk
1/8 tsp. red pepper
¼ tsp. salt

In saucepan, blend flour and butter. Meanwhile, bring milk to a boil; add all at once to flour mixture, stirring until smooth. Add chives, cream, and other seasonings. Serve hot on toast.

Crayfish

Fresh crayfish
Salt

Pepper
Sauce (optional)

Locate some crayfish or fresh water "crabs" as they are sometimes known, in a lake, pond or stream. Take them home alive in a pail or wash tub. Fill the tub or pail with fresh water when you get home and throw in a handful of salt in the water. Leave them in the salty water for 10 minutes. Heat a large kettle of boiling water and add a little salt and pepper to it. When the water is boiling, drop the crayfish alive into the water. Let them boil 3 minutes after they turn a beautiful red color Just like a cooked lobster. Remove them from the water and let them cool. When they are cool, shuck the skin from the tails and you will have the finest shrimp meat. Serve the meat from the tails cold or hot and with any sauce or butter.

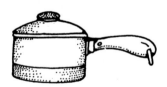

Baked Eel

Skin eel, split and take back bone out. Cut into 2 to 3 inch pieces. Wash in plenty of salted water. Drain and dry. Dredge in flour, season with paprika, salt, and pepper. Place in greased baking pan. Bake at 400° until brown.

Stewed Eel

1½-3 lbs. eel
1½ qts. water
6 T. vinegar
4 cloves
2 tsp. chopped parsley

½ sliced lemon
10 peppercorns
3 bay leaves
½ onion (sliced)

Skin the eel by pulling skin from head to tail in 2-inch sections. Clean each section separately. Pull out membrane and push out intestines with handle of wooden spoon. Rub inside with salt and rinse several times with clean water. Bring the 1½ qts. water and vinegar to boil; scald pieces of eel in water; drain. In saucepan, put eel and remaining ingredients and cover eel with water. Bring to a boil and simmer for 15 minutes; drain. Serve eel with hot butter and lemon juice and wedges.

Frog Legs

Skin the froglegs, wash, and cut off feet. Soak at least 1 hour in salt water. Lightly beat egg. Season legs with salt and pepper. Dip in cornmeal (or bread crumbs), then in egg and again in cornmeal. Fry in deep hot fat. Drain fat before serving.

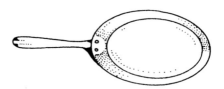

Fried Frog Legs

¼ C. butter or margarine
2 lbs. frog legs
Salt and white pepper, to taste

¼ C. flour or cornmeal
   (may mix both together)
1 tsp. grated onion

Dry legs with paper towel. Mix salt, pepper, and flour mixture; coat frog legs. Fry in hot butter until browned, add onion for 5 minutes before frog legs are done and browned. Cover and cook for 15 to 18 minutes more or until tender. Serve hot. Serves 3 to 5.

Leg Roast from Big Critters

6 lbs. hind leg roast
¼ C. butter
4-5 sprigs parsley (minced)
½ tsp. dry savory (crumbled)
½ tsp. dried tarragon (crumbled)
1 C. red wine or part wine &
*   game stock*

10-12 juniper berries (crushed)
Salt and pepper
¼ C. currant jelly
½ C. red wine
1 T. brandy
1½ T. roux or flour

Melt butter; add herbs. Cook for several minutes. Place roast seasoned with salt and pepper and lightly sprinkled with flour in roasting pan. Pour butter over crust and place in preheated 450° oven. In 20 minutes reduce heat to 325°. Add wine and stock. Cover and roast for 25 minutes per pound, basting frequently. When tender, remove to heated platter and keep warm while preparing sauce. For Sauce: Add 1 C. stock to juices in roaster. Stir to loosen all bits in pan. Strain into small saucepan. Add jelly, ½ C. wine, and roux. Stir until sauce is smooth and thickened. Allow to simmer a few minutes. Pour into heated gravy boat. If juniper berries aren't found in your area, write to an herb and spice company. You can substitute equal parts of gin and stock for the wine.

Chapter XIII

MAKING MEETINGS FUN

Besides all the fresh air and the good dose of vitamin whatever-it-is that you get out of sunshine, there's another real advantage of doing your hunting in the nude.

And that the fact that nude hunters are not very attractive to chiggers. Those microscopic little pesks always seem

o

In the very center of this circle
you will find a chigger
magnified 400 times.

to settle in on folks around their belts, socks, or wherever else the clothing tends to be snug.

Any of those pesky chiggers that lands on a nude hunter can look all he wants for where the clothes are snug ... he ain't gonna find any 'cause there ain't no clothes.

That speck-on-a-speck of a little critter will bail off in disgust, waiting for someone foolish enough to be wearing clothes. He'll much prefer someone to come along with a nice tight sock, or a snug ~~brazier~~ ... ~~brasz~~ ... ~~brasser~~ ... ~~brassai~~ ... ~~brasseri~~ ... some snug whaddacallit strap.

Just to kind of get an on-the-spot understanding of the situation, just wait 'til the next hunting season, then some Monday morning when you're all having a meeting at work — just look around you; you'll see what I mean.

Lloyd, from Accounts Receivable, will be scratching his ankles around the top of his socks like he's gonna scratch 'em right off. Tanya from Receiving is secretly working around on her shoulder, attempting to get the itching to stop. Down at the other end of the table, Jim Thorne from Engineering will be pretending to tuck his shirt tail in as he proceeds to lay waste to some chigger holed up in a little red spot just northeast of his belly button.

On the other hand, if you've been doing your weekend hunting in the nude, you can relax. It'll be kind of fun playing a little game that your foresight enables you to do.

Just about the time there's a lull in the scratching you might come up with a comment about "how bad the chiggers are this year."

That's almost guaranteed to bring on an itching frenzy around the whole table. With just the right timing, you can stop Marc Jensen right in the middle of his carefully rehearsed pie chart presentation, right in midair.

Who says that all business meetings have to be dull and lifeless?

Muskrat Fricassee

1 qt. water
1 dressed muskrat, 1-1½ lb.)
¼ C. flour
1 T. salt
¼ tsp. pepper

¼ C. shortening
¾ C. water
1/16 tsp. red pepper
1 large onion (sliced)
2 tsp. salt

(Note: Be sure to remove all glands from muskrat before cooking. These glands lie under the body and are light yellow. Also between the forelegs, between the shoulders, back and under the thighs. Cut these out carefully.)

With damp cloth, wipe muskrat, pick off hair, cut across back and below ribs. Put in glass or enamel bowl, add salt and water to cover. Refrigerate overnight. Drain and rinse muskrat in clear water. Cut in pieces and roll in peppers, salt, and flour. Place coated pieces in heavy skillet; brown slowly. Sprinkle the brown pieces with paprika. Add onion, cooked until slightly yellow and transparent. Add ½ C. water and simmer for 20 to 30 minutes. May need to add more water. Makes 2 to 3 servings.

Fried Muskrat

1 qt. water
1 large dressed muskrat
1 onion (large)
½ tsp. poultry seasoning
1½ tsp. salt
½ C. milk

1 egg
1 tsp. salt
¼ tsp. thyme
¾ C. flour
⅓ C. shortening
Water

With damp cloth, wipe muskrat clean of hair. Cut across back and below the ribs. Put into glass or enamel bowl. Cover with salt water (1 T. salt to 1 qt. water). Refrgerate overnight. Drain and rinse in clear water. Place in kettle and add water, salt, poultry seasoning, and onion; simmer for 20 minutes. Remove parboiled muskrat, cut into serving pieces. Beat flour, milk, and eggs; add salt and thyme. Dip muskrat in batter and brown slowly. Add ¼ C. water, cover, and simmer 20 minutes. Remove, cover, and cook for 15 to 20 minutes until crisp. Makes 2 to 4 servings.

EPILOGUE

So it goes. Nude hunters have things to consider that the more traditionally clad hunters are never faced with.

But the joys of hunting au naturel are worth the few little inconveniences one encounters.

Happy hunting!!

Need a Gift?

For

• Shower • Birthday • Mother's Day •
• Anniversary • Christmas •

Turn Page For Order Form
(Order Now While Supply Lasts!)

TO ORDER COPIES OF

HUNTING IN THE NUDE COOKBOOK

Please send me _____copies of
Hunting in the Nude Cookbook at $9.95 each
plus $3.00 shipping and handling per book.
(Make checks payable to **Quixote Press.**)

Name_____

Street_____

City _____ State_____ Zip _____

Send Orders To:
Quixote Press
3544 Blakslee St.
Wever, IA 52658
1-800-571-2665

TO ORDER COPIES OF

HUNTING IN THE NUDE COOKBOOK

Please send me _____copies of
Hunting in the Nude Cookbook at $9.95 each
plus $3.00 shipping and handling per book.
(Make checks payable to **Quixote Press.**)

Name_____

Street_____

City _____ State_____ Zip _____

Send Orders To:
Quixote Press
3544 Blakslee St.
Wever, IA 52658
1-800-571-2665